SOCIAL SKILLS FOR KIDS

A PRE-SCHOOL SUCCESS TOOLKIT: PRACTICAL STRATEGIES FROM A SPEECH THERAPIST FOR YOUR TODDLER TO MAKE FRIENDS, IMPROVE BEHAVIOUR AND COMMUNICATION, EVEN DELAYED SKILLS WON'T HOLD THEM BACK!

KIDS SLT PUBLICATIONS

Copyright Kids SLT Publications 2023 – All rights reserved.

The content contained within this book may not be reproduced, duplicated, or transmitted without direct written permission from the author or the publisher.

Under no circumstances will any blame or legal responsibility be held against the publisher, or author, for any damages, reparation, or monetary loss due to the information contained within this book. Either directly or indirectly. You are responsible for your own choices, actions and results.

Legal Notice

This book is copyright protected. This book is only for personal use. You cannot amend, distribute, sell, use, quote, or paraphrase any part, or the content within this book, without the consent of the author or publisher.

Disclaimer Notice

Please note the information contained within this document is for educational and entertainment purposes only. All effort has been executed to present accurate, up to date, and reliable, complete information. No warranties of any kind are declared or implied. Readers acknowledge that the author is not engaging in the rendering of legal, financial, medical, or professional advice. The content within this book has been derived from various sources. Please consult a licensed professional before attempting any techniques outlined in this book.

By reading this document, the reader agrees that under no circumstances is the author responsible for any losses, direct or indirect, which are incurred as a result of the use of the information contained within this document, including, but not limited to, errors, omissions, or inaccuracies.

CONTENTS

Introduction   7

1. GETTING USED TO THE EDUCATIONAL SYSTEM   13
   What Exactly Is Preschool?   14
   Questions to Ask Preschools   16
   When to Apply For a Preschool Place   19
   Advice For Those Outside The UK   20

2. INTRODUCING THE CONCEPT OF PRESCHOOL   27
   How to Write Your Own Social Story   29
   Social Story For The First Day of Preschool   30
   Comic Strip to Introduce a Teacher   32
   Time For a Walk   35
   Other Ideas to Introduce Preschool   37
   Getting "Special" Clothes Ready   38

3. A TYPICAL DAY IN PRESCHOOL   41
   Activities   42
   Nap Time   47
   Indoor vs. Outdoor Play   48
   Snacks   49
   Making Friends   51
   A Typical Day Social Story and Comic Strip   52

4. HELP AVAILABLE FOR CHILDREN WITH LEARNING DELAYS AND DISORDERS 55
   Delays and Disorders That Cause Concern 56
   Early Intervention Is Crucial 58
   What Are IEPs and EHCPs 59
   Visual Support 61
   Audio Support 63
   Sign Language vs Makaton 67
   A Social Story and Comic Strip For Additional Needs 68

5. HOW TO PREPARE YOUR LITTLE ONE FOR PRESCHOOL 71
   The Beauty of Routine 71
   Teaching Independence 74
   Learning How to Play 76
   Leading By Example With Communication 80
   Ditch the Dummy (Pacifier) 81
   Getting Everyone Involved 83
   Use a Visual Calendar 83
   Teaching Manners With a Social Story and Comic Strip 84

6. KEEPING UP THE COMMUNICATION 87
   Super Important Communication 88
   The Usual Lines of Communication In Preschool 88
   Modern Ways to Communicate With Your Child's Teacher 91
   Communication For Those With Additional Needs 92
   Finding Support By Communicating With Other Parents 94
   How to Help Little Ones Communicate With a Social Story and Comic Strip 96

7. DEALING WITH UNPLEASANT
   BEHAVIOURAL ISSUES — 99
   Refusing to Tidy — 100
   Throwing Things — 101
   Telling Lies — 102
   The Preschool Attitude — 104
   Temper Tantrums — 105
   Violence or Aggression Towards Others — 107
   Reducing Negative Behaviours Through
   Social Stories and Comic Strips — 110

8. DEALING WITH BIG EMOTIONS AND
   MELTDOWNS — 113
   Getting Good at Emotional Awareness
   at Home — 116
   What Causes a Meltdown — 119
   How to Help Your Child Cope With
   Stress and Anxiety — 121
   Separation Anxiety — 123
   Mindfulness and Meditation For
   Children — 124
   Anger Management Through a Social
   Story and Comic Strip — 127

   Conclusion — 129
   References — 135

INTRODUCTION

Let's start with the question, who can remember their first day of school? How old were you? Was it a positive experience? I wonder if your experience, positive or negative, impacts the way you take your child on their first day!

I can't remember much but I know that I sat at a table and I started to colour with mum standing behind me. The moment I went to show her, I turned around and she had disappeared. There is something about this experience that is often burned into our minds.

Over the years…okay, decades, since I started school, things have changed so much in the educational system and most for the better. With more and more women entering full-time work, the need for children to start preschool has increased. So, instead of children starting their first day of school around the age of 5, they are starting preschool at 2 or 3 years old.

It's incredibly hard for little minds to adapt to such a big change when they are so comfortable in their routine with their caregiver. This is even more of a challenge if your child has any kind of developmental delay or disorder.

Meeting new people, listening to the teacher, following instructions, having to share, and perhaps even eating in preschool are all things that can seem overwhelming for a little person. It's a little bit like starting a new job, but you have the added years of experience to handle social interactions.

Such young minds are still working on these skills and the frustration and confusion that may come about from this massive change can bring about a whole set of other problems. All of a sudden, your child who slept 12 hours a night is now bouncing off the walls until 11 p.m. Your pride in a potty-trained toddler is dashed away by unexpected accidents.

But there is a bright side. Preschool teaches children how to adjust, provides more opportunities to play and supports social and emotional development. With minds that act like sponges, children get to explore more of the world around them.

So, how can we make this transition easier for children, particularly atypical children who are going to need additional help, guidance, and love?

Preparation! Preparation for you and for your child. As an adult, we know that if we are aware of what is to be expected and what is required of us, we feel more confident about entering a different and unknown situation. The same applies to the world of education. And when your child is more aware of what preschool is, the transition will be smoother.

As a parent, you are about to learn how to find the best preschool that matches the needs of your child and family. You will understand the roles of different educational specialists and how they support your child throughout the day. You will discover important techniques to improve communication between everyone involved, and what to do when emotions become too much for your little one to handle.

What's more, you will be armed with tones of techniques to prepare your child, like how to adapt routines so that school and home are more in-sync, how to start getting them used to the idea of going to preschool, how to get better at emotional regulation, even at their young age, and how to make friends.

There are a number of ways that we can do this and two of my favourite ways to help children are through social stories and comic strip conversations.

Social stories are a learning tool that were originally created for people on the autistic spectrum and are now widely used to help all children. The stories contain information on a specific topic and is then presented to the reader in a safe way. Imagine you have to take your child to the doctor for the first time. Reading them a story about what to expect in a meaningful way. Some social stories have pictures, others have spaces where you can add photos of your own environment. (mention original source for social stories)

Comic strip conversations function in a similar way, a learning tool to help prepare children for upcoming social situations and events. The slight difference is that comic strips prepare children for conversations whereas social stories are more about the situation.

In the case of preparing children for their first day, a social story would prepare them for the events. A comic strip would prepare them for a conversation with their new teacher. So, you can see how they work well together.

This is relevant because, throughout the book, you will find several examples of social stories and templates for comic strips that you can use with your children. There will be a chapter on both learning tools, and in more detail so that you learn how to create them, or feel free to use mine.

Many of you who have read my previous books will know that I am far from an artist. My cartoon comics are stick people. If you are more creative than me, that's awesome. And if you are at the same artistic level as me and stick people are your limit, that's great too! The emphasis is on the words rather than the creativity.

Similarly with social stories, every family is different. Please feel free to use my stories, use them as inspiration, or create your own from scratch. I haven't included any images because I am a firm believer in photos that are relevant and bring more meaning to the story, but you will also find tips on how to get these photos before the first day of preschool.

As a speech and language therapist and a mum, I fully understand that you are up to your eyeballs in stress, jobs, and responsibilities. I promise that this book will be practical, easy to use, and relevant to all backgrounds and cultural differences. Above all, I want to make sure that each and every mum, dad, and caregiver can feel confident in their parenting skills.

Let's begin by taking a closer look at preschool education, the available services, and matching the needs of your child to the educational environment that is going to bring out the best in them.

1

GETTING USED TO THE EDUCATIONAL SYSTEM

Without putting any pressure on a parent, deciding on a preschool is definitely a major decision we have to make. Research has shown that high-quality early childhood education and care (ECEC) has a positive effect on a child's education, cognition, behaviour, and social outcomes (UK Parliament, 2021). For many parents, the education system is unknown territory, not knowing the process or what to expect. For the first time, you will be entrusting someone else with the care of your child, and this is daunting. So, before we start looking at how to prepare children, let's start with what parents need to know.

WHAT EXACTLY IS PRESCHOOL?

A preschool is a place for children between the ages of 3 and 5 who aren't old enough to start school. Most children in the UK start school in September after their 4th birthday. In the US, the age is between 4 and 6; however, in countries in Asia, vary between the age of 5 and 7.

You may have heard some people refer to preschool as nursery, and while there are some overlaps, they are actually different. Nurseries take children as young as 6 weeks old. They work on a full-time or part-time basis and are open for longer hours so that parents are able to work, including during the summer. Nurseries can be either private or a school nursery, one that is part of a primary school.

On the contrary, preschool is often used more as a preparation for starting school. Children often attend either the morning or afternoon session, staying for 2 or 3 hours at a time.

Finally, both nurseries and preschools have to follow the national curriculum, a set of subjects and standards set by the government for primary and secondary schools, with the intention that all children are learning the same content. This means that regardless of what you choose, children get to follow a structure that also supports their transition into primary school. All early years education providers have to follow the Early Years Foundation Stage (EYFS) part of the national curriculum. To make sure you are familiar with this side of education in the UK, all childcare providers, whether registered childcare providers or a school, are regulated by Ofsted (Office for Standards in Education, Children's Services and Skills).

Many primary schools have a nursery school or preschool. From here on in, we will use the term preschool for both. Although we are getting ahead of ourselves a little, it is a good idea to look into these educational providers, especially if you are concerned that your child may be atypical. The transition from preschool to primary school is smoother as they will be going to the same centre (but possibly a different building), and many of their friends may move up into primary school with them.

While you are able to choose a preschool, it's not the same when it comes to primary school. The primary school your child attends is determined by the local authorities depending on set criteria, usually based on the distance between the home and the school. In most cases, the parent's wishes are taken into consideration, and the child gets to attend the school of their choice unless they are 'oversubscribed' and there are more applicants than places.

Let's bring it back to the here and now. To get a better feel for a preschool and whether your child will be happy, it's a good idea to visit various locations before settling on one. And for these visits, you will want to have a list of questions ready.

QUESTIONS TO ASK PRESCHOOLS

First off, you should check the qualifications of the teachers. Typical qualifications include Qualified Teacher Status, Early Years Professional Status, and Early Years Teacher Status, though there are other qualifications, especially if a teacher has come from overseas. Within the qualifications, there are levels set by the Regulated Qualifications Framework (RQF). There are 8 levels. Levels 1 and 2 refer to GCSE qualifications and level 3 to A-level certificates. When we get to level 5, we have foundation degrees and a Diploma in higher education (DipHE), level 6 for a Bachelor's degree, 7 for a Master's degree, and level 8 for doctorates and PhDs.

Aside from their qualifications, it is wise to ask about experience. Teaching is one of those jobs where qualifications are only a fraction of the job. You don't want a teacher who is super qualified but lacks compassion and empathy! You should also double-check that the preschool is Ofsted registered.

A teacher's qualifications impact the EYFS ratio, the number of children per adult in the class. For children over 3 in preschools, the ratio is 1 teacher to 13 children when the teacher has a suitable level 6 qualification. When there is no level 6 qualification, the ratio is 1:8. Of course, there will be more than one adult in the classroom, so ask questions about the other supervisors that will be involved with providing care.

Children are entitled to 15 hours of free childcare. This doesn't sound like much when you consider a 40-hour working week. Ask the preschool if they have the option of 30 hours a week and the costs. Some families are eligible for 30 hours of free care depending on criteria such as income, the child's circumstances, and immigration status as some examples. As you are working out your budget, check that the preschool is registered so that you can register for tax-free childcare.

The next questions on your list should be related to safety and how they ensure children are safe in both indoor and outdoor areas. Check their accident protocols because all accidents should be logged along with any medication that was given.

Preschools will often have a behaviour policy, and it will be useful to know how they handle bad behaviour. Ideally, the preschool will use positive reinforcements such as stickers for good behaviour rather than relying on punishing the bad.

Finally, there will be information to find out about day-to-day practices. What type of activities do they organise, and how this supports children's learning and development? What kind of snacks are available or lunch if they stay for longer? By three, most children are less reliant on a nap, but there might be a space for resting or quiet time.

Although the advice on choosing a preschool is based on the UK system, these are fundamental questions for any country. Let's recap the questions:

- How many teachers and children are in the class?
- What qualifications do the adults have?
- How many hours are available?
- What costs are involved?
- Is there financial support available?
- What safety practices are in place?
- What is the behaviour policy?
- What activities are there?
- What snacks/lunches are offered?

- Do we pay for the snacks/milk?
- Is there a uniform?
- Do the children have a nap?

The final part of the process is to see if there are any orientation days where you and your child can visit the school and spend a little time in the classroom. This will give you more time to see how the teachers interact with the children and, of course, how your child interacts in the environment.

WHEN TO APPLY FOR A PRESCHOOL PLACE

It may seem like an exaggeration in the films when pregnant women start to stress about choosing the right care for their children, but in some cases, it is the way. This is particularly true for private nurseries, and there can be waiting lists from 6 months to a year.

The first place to contact will be your local authorities for the application process. You will find that application dates open in January and are closed by the end of February for those who want to start in the September of the same year.

So, although you may not actually be pregnant and start to find a preschool, it really doesn't hurt to get a head start on the process.

ADVICE FOR THOSE OUTSIDE THE UK

In the perfect world, I would have the same specific advice for every country. Our Facebook community, 'Kids' Delayed Speech and Language Support Group, has over 6,400 members and counting from all over the world, and I try to provide information that will help everyone. However, as my career is in the UK and this is where I have experience in schools, I am only qualified to talk about what happens here.

I have researched where to find advice for some other countries. I'm sorry if your country isn't mentioned, but the best place is to start with your country's government website or your local authorities.

In the US

Preschool in the US is considered two years of childcare before a child starts kindergarten. Children are normally 3 by the December of the academic year. Some parents whose children were born after the 1st of September prefer to delay the start of preschool until the next year.

There tends to be more of a focus on preschool readiness in the US. You might want to check your child's level of self-care, whether they are potty trained (or close), if they can wash their hands, and put on their shoes and coat. It's helpful if their speech is understandable, that they can follow simple directions, and they can handle transitions and be away from their primary caregivers.

The cost may be upsetting for those who have seen what is available in the UK. The costs will vary a lot from state to state. The average cost is $889 per month or $10,668 per year. In Arizona, it could be $787 per month, but in Washington D.C. is approximately $1,372 (Cadence Education, 2021).

Some states have started to offer free pre-K services, so again, check with your local authorities first. Definitely start as soon as possible because, as you can imagine, there are waiting lists. The federal program, Head Start, offers free pre-K across all states but for families that are below the poverty level, children in foster care, and families that receive public assistance.

In Australia and New Zealand

Preschool in Australia generally starts when the child turns 4, and primary school begins when they are 6. Most preschools are attached to a primary school and follow the same hours and timetable, so 9 a.m. to 3 p.m. and open during term time. There are some that offer extended hours from 7 a.m. to 6 p.m. for those who need it.

For children aged 3 to 6, the minimum teacher-to-child ratio is 1:10. Preschools follow the Early Years Learning Framework, which focuses on learning through play and stories and transitioning to primary school.

When it comes to fees, it gets more complicated and very much depends on the territory. For example, the Australian capital and South Australia have no fees, but preschools may ask for a voluntary contribution. New South Wales, Queensland, and Victoria have fees, often set by the providers, and the Northern Territory, South Australia, Tasmania, and Western Australia have no fees. There are some crazy waiting lists, so start planning and contacting local authorities as soon as possible, even a year in advance!

Those living in New Zealand have an excellent choice of early childhood education (ECE), with over 5,000 centres across the country (ENZ, 2020). Teacher-led centres are known as kindergartens or 'Te Kura', school playgroups. Playcenter and playgroups are parent-led. 95% of children aged 3 to the day before their 6th birthday are entitled to 20-22 hours of free ECE. Furthermore, ECE preschools in New Zealand work through the school holidays.

What I love most about New Zealand is the curriculum, known as Te Whāriki, which very much encourages parent involvement in the child's learning. Parents can visit centres, take part in activities, and regularly talk to teachers. Most centres have a digital camera or web camera. Children can choose pieces of their work to show parents throughout the day, and a portfolio of their work is made to take to primary school with them.

These preschools are in high demand, so once again, get in there as soon as you can by contacting authorities or the preschool in your area.

In Europe

Each country and even region will have its own differences but preschool in Europe follows the early childhood education and care (ECEC) system governed by the European Union. This system has a framework of 5 components:

- Access to early childhood education and care
- Training and working conditions of staff in charge of ECEC
- Definition of appropriate curricula
- Governance and funding
- Monitoring and evaluation systems

(European Union, N.D.)

Thanks to this framework, 95% of children aged 4 are in some form of early childhood education and care.

Again, each country will have its own criteria for fees depending on a family or parent's situation. France may have been one of the first countries to offer free early years care. Preschools first opened in the 1830s, and for low-income families, it was free. Today, preschools are free for the ages of 3 to 6. In Berlin, Germany, the last year before primary school is free, with parents paying for food and certain activities. Sweden and Finland, often seen as the examples of childcare in Europe, have fees depending on income. Low-income families have access to free preschool, whereas the top end of fees is capped at 147€ and 290€ for those better off. We can forgive Finland for being more expensive because children can have 40 hours of free preschool.

In South Asia

South Asia consists of Brunei, Burna, Cambodia, Timor-Leste, India, Indonesia, Laos, Malaysia, Pakistan, the Phillippines, Singapore, Thailand, and Vietnam. South Asia has various difficulties with education, and these were made worse by Covid. UNICEF estimated that 22 million children in South

Asia missed out on early childhood education (UNICEF, 2020). A lack of funding is another large issue which means many children, especially girls, don't get to attend school, let alone early years education.

Let's look at a few countries in more detail. In South Asia, preschool is known as kindergarten.

In Thailand, kindergarten is available for children aged 3 to 7. The curriculum is based on the alphabet, numbers, crafts, stories, and playing. They also learn about patriotic values, religions, and the Thai monarchy. Kindergarten is free unless parents want to take the child to an international school.

Indonesia has 49,000 kindergartens, and 99% of those are private, with prices ranging from £30 to £5,300 per month for international kindergartens (Education Destination Asia, N.D.). Children follow a rich curriculum, including things like moral education and physical activities. In Vietnam, the focus of kindergarten for children aged 4 and 5 is more play-based. Most of the centres offer free early education, but there will be fees for certain things.

Malaysia is an example of how different kindergartens are. Public preschools spend more time developing social and emotional skills. The goal of private preschools is more cognitive development and helping children reach their goals. Fees are difficult to list because of the sheer difference in school and the different materials.

Obviously, last but not least, my home country, Pakistan! There is free preschool education for children aged 3 to 5, but it isn't always easy to get a place with many preschools oversubscribed. In this case, people may have to look at international preschools. The National ECCE curriculum allows for the physical, social, emotional, cognitive, and moral development of children.

The best advice for those who are outside of the UK is to contact your local authorities to find out exactly what is available in terms of hours, fees, and curriculum. While you are there, check about waiting lists and the process so you don't get caught off-guard when preschool starts.

It's not until you have settled on a preschool, regardless of your country, that you can start preparing your little one for what's to come. Well done on this big decision, and now let's move our attention back to the children and these all-important social stories.

2

INTRODUCING THE CONCEPT OF PRESCHOOL

Think about the process of moving house. You have a couple of months of getting used to the idea, plenty of packing, and of course, you have been to your new home to see it. Everyone has their new rooms chosen, and you have probably even planned your new route to school and work. Your brain has had time to adjust. You wouldn't think twice about talking to your child about the new house in order to make the transition smoother. The same thinking should be applied to school.

Up until now, your child has spent the majority of time with you. You understand them. They know the rules and routine, and there is no such thing as separation anxiety. Making a change to preschool, even if it is just a few hours a day, can completely disrupt everything they are used to. For children who have communication delays or disorders, expecting them to communicate with new friends and teachers is a tall order. The same can be said for children who are more dependent on their routines and struggle to switch from one task to another.

All children need time to get used to the idea of starting preschool, and some will need more time and support than others. It is recommended to start talking about preschool a few weeks, even a couple of months before the start date as well as other strategies to normalize the concept.

There are dozens of books to read to children on the first day of school, and naturally, these are a good place to start. But social stories are custom-made creations to prepare children for events they need to expect. A story about Jack and Jill going to school normalizes the first day. A story that includes your child's name is going to provide much deeper meaning.

Social stories can introduce social skills, positively change behaviours, and reduce a child's anxiety. But because they are more personal, it is worth taking some time to create your own.

HOW TO WRITE YOUR OWN SOCIAL STORY

The first step and most essential is to put yourself in the shoes of your audience. For example, if your child is autistic, it's a case of getting literally down to their level and seeing the challenges of the first day at school through their eyes. As an adult, you would introduce yourself to the teacher. Through the child's eyes, it's crucial to address the issue they would have, whether that's social anxiety or communication issues. If they have particular food challenges, your social story should look more into snacktime and what to expect.

The goal of our story is to introduce children to the first day of preschool. But this won't always be the case. Once you have seen how beneficial social stories are, you might find yourself keen to make more, like for a doctor's visit or the first time on an aeroplane. Be clear on what you want to achieve.

The next step is to collect all the information you need. In terms of preschool, you will have to visit first, and this is the ideal opportunity to gather as much accurate information as you can. This will include things like the teachers' names, the activities in the classroom, what is in the playground, the toilets and sinks, what snacks are given, and so on. I can't stress this enough, if your child has any form of social stress or anxiety, ask if you can take photos and let the school know that you are making a social story. If you can't get photos, you can draw images, print basic images and include a photo of your child for visual cues.

Once you have all the information, it's time to write the text in an age-appropriate way. For 3 to 4-year-olds, it's best to stick to one sentence per page with positive and reassuring language, never guaranteeing anything you aren't sure of. Make sure your social stories answer the who, what, why, when, and where of a situation or behaviour and are always written in the first person so it's read from the student's perspective.

SOCIAL STORY FOR THE FIRST DAY OF PRESCHOOL

From personal experience, it is not always easy to get in touch with your creative side, and it's even harder to find the time. If you are desperate to start using a social story now, You can take some pieces of paper, fold them in half and copy the following lines onto each page. If you haven't had time to take photos, jump online and type in the name of the preschool, you will be surprised how many images pop up, and the preschool may even have a website that has some images.

My story uses Mum as an example. Please don't take this as an assumption of mine because today, there are a number of possibilities for who will take a child to school. It just saves me listing every family member, friend, or childminder in a rather repetitive way. You can adapt the story to your situation. In my story, we walk, you may need to take the car or bus, and you may even have to drop someone else off first. Oh, and don't forget a fun, appealing front cover to catch your child's interest!

- Page 1: Today is my first day of preschool. It will be fun, but I am a little nervous too.
- Page 2: I will get dressed (uniform if required) and have my breakfast.
- Page 3: I will clean my teeth, wash my face, and brush my hair (mum helps if necessary)
- Page 4: I am going to walk to preschool with my mum.
- Page 5: At preschool, we will go into the playground, and my teacher (name) will be there.
- Page 6: There will be other children. We will go to class together.
- Page 7: In the classroom, we will sit in a circle, and (teacher's name) will talk to us.

- Page 8: There are lots of books in the classroom. We will listen to a story.
- Page 9: Next, there will be time for us to play. There are lots of toys in the classroom, like (list some examples)
- Page 10: We will go to the toilet and wash our hands.
- Page 11: After we wash our hands, there will be a snack. (List examples of snacks).
- Page 12: When we finish our snack, we will play in the playground.
- Page 13: Then, it will be time to go inside the classroom and line up.
- Page 14: Mum will pick me up from preschool, and we will walk home together.

From my example, you can see why it is so beneficial to collect as much information as you can before writing the story. The more details you have, the more prepared your child will feel.

COMIC STRIP TO INTRODUCE A TEACHER

Usually, comic strips are used with children who can read and write because they can make them themselves, but I would still use them for younger children by keeping the conversation simple. Children who can read and write can create their own comic strip conversations with a little guidance. There are some basic techniques that need to be used, in particular with the types of speech bubbles.

For example, when words are meant to be spoken loudly, they are bigger and quite small. If a group of people are talking together, the stick people share the same speech bubble. If the speech bubbles overlap, it means that someone has interrupted the other person's speech.

Furthermore, colours can be used to highlight different emotional aspects of a conversation. Speech bubbles with different coloured outlines mean the following:

- Green: Good ideas, friendly, happy
- Red: Bad ideas, unfriendly, angry
- Blue: Sad and uncomfortable feelings
- Yellow: Scared
- Black: Facts and the truth
- Orange: Questions
- Brown: Comfort
- Purple: Pride
- Multicoloured: Confusion

For younger children, I wouldn't go over the top with colours and rather than explaining what each colour means, and you can talk about the feelings that the stick person might be having. They will start to associate the colours with the meanings, plus it makes the comic strip more engaging!

Remember that comic strip conversations, like social stories, need to have an objective. This objective could be to prepare for a difficult situation that is making the child anxious, solve a problem, help your little one communicate their feelings, or look at a possible future situation in a non-threatening way.

Again, my example is very basic, and my drawing abilities go no further than stick people with some facial expressions! You are more than welcome to print mine to use or create your own based on mine. And again, if your child has a specific issue, the issue needs to be addressed. The child in my story is incredibly shy, so our objective is to help them feel safe about meeting their new teacher.

TIME FOR A WALK

Ok, so it's not necessarily a walk, but it is a few trips to preschool before your little one actually begins the new routine. I would even take advantage of these visits by going a few times, and this is especially handy if the preschool is on the way to another location, like a supermarket or petrol station.

If the school is en route to another location, point it out each time you go past. Let them know that this is going to be their new school, that they are going to have lots of fun, there are lots of toys and games to play, and that they will be able to make new friends.

Next, make a more purposeful trip to the preschool. If your plan is to walk there, then go for a walk to preschool. If it's any other type of transport, try your hardest to make these visits using the same transport so that they begin to experience part of the new routine.

Visit the preschool at different times of the day. It's good to see the preschool when the children are in the playground when they are in class and even when the parents are picking the children up and dropping them off. All of these visits will prepare your little one for different times of the day.

Pay close attention to their reactions so that you can address possible concerns in social stories and comic strip conversations. If your child becomes clinging when they are watching parents drop their children off, it might mean you need to work on separation anxiety. On the other hand, if they are excited when watching the children in the playground, you use this moment as a reminder of the good times they will have.

Aside from these moments, there should also be an official visit where you and your child can visit the preschool and spend some time there. You should be able to meet the teacher together, explore the classroom, and play on the playground together.

OTHER IDEAS TO INTRODUCE PRESCHOOL

Starting preschool could be a huge social change for many children, especially if they don't have siblings or cousins that they spend a lot of time with. Without these social interactions, children may find it hard to fit into a classroom environment and start making friends.

As soon as you can, start making sure your little one has as many opportunities to be around children of a similar age. This can be as simple as going to a park together. You may have to break out of your comfort zone and make friends with other parents in order to have some play dates. It would be exceptionally helpful if you could arrange a play date with someone who will be in the same class as your child.

Role play is the perfect opportunity to get your child used to new routines that will start during preschool. You can have "carpet time" when your child sits in a circle with some of their toys and have story time together. You can switch roles and let your child be the teacher, and they can choose a song or even hand out the snacks.

Start turning independence into a game. Hang their backpack in the wrong place and get them to hang it in the right place. Have races for putting jackets and shoes on. Have them put jumpers and coats on cuddly toys so they can practice buttons and zips, or ask them if they can help you with your buttons and zips. All of these are skills that will help them in preschool.

Finally, it's wise to start their new routine a few weeks before preschool begins, more specifically, their bedtime routine. They may have to start waking up earlier, so they should start going to bed earlier. If your little one is still having a nap, now is a good time to start weaning them off it. Yes, there will be a few grumpy moments, even days, but having this routine in place will mean less tiredness when preschool starts. If you know the transition is going to be difficult, you will also know that having a tired little one starting school is going to be more challenging for everyone.

GETTING "SPECIAL" CLOTHES READY

Put yourself in a teacher's shoes for a minute. You have 20 children, not all being fully potty trained, but all of them wearing awkward jeans with buttons. That's 20 buttons for the teacher. Now it's too hot, and the children all want their jumpers off, but yes, there are more buttons. Then, there are 20 little shoes with 40 shoe laces for the teacher to tie! Rather than doing fun, educational activities with the class, the teacher spends half their time becoming the master of buttons and laces!

All clothes should be easy for the children, above all, clothes that they can pull down and pull up so that they can go to the bathroom by themselves. Velcro shoes are perfect. And of course, the children need to be comfortable.

At the same time, having "special" clothes for school can add to the sense of being a big girl/boy going to a big school. Have a drawer in their room dedicated to school clothes and let them choose some items to go in the special drawer. Explain what types of clothes should go in the drawer so that they have a nice range of comfortable, easy clothes.

In these weeks before starting preschool, you also have the opportunity to start talking about what will happen during a typical day at preschool. For this, you will need to learn more about what types of things teachers plan to do with children. Naturally, every preschool will have its own plan, but there are certain things that are likely to occur in all.

3

A TYPICAL DAY IN PRESCHOOL

When people asked me about what superpower I would like to have, I always said I would like to be invisible. Not to play tricks on people or even rob a bank, but just to be able to watch my children in school and see exactly what they never tell us. While on that topic, don't be surprised if you ask your child what they did at preschool and they say "nothing". I still remember that for the first two weeks of my youngest in preschool, apparently, the only thing she did in preschool was eat. It took two months to get to "eat and play". Don't worry; during a typical day in preschool, your little one will be plenty busy, and you will see this in their tiredness!

ACTIVITIES

The activities that children take part in are based on the seven areas of learning and development set out by the EYFS curriculum (or the corresponding curriculum in your country). In England, we have three prime areas: communication and language, physical development, and personal, social and emotional development. These prime areas are supported by four specific areas: literacy, mathematics, understanding the world, and expressive arts and designs. We will take a look at each of these in more detail with examples of possible activities.

Communication and language

Spoken language is the foundation for all areas of learning and development. The goal of preschool teachers is to create an environment that is rich in language. This is done through conversations, stories, rhymes, poems, and role play. Ideas of activities include:

- Picture books
- Puzzle books
- Dressing up box
- Puppet shows

- Card games (matching vocabulary)
- Stone stories

Physical development

Physical activities help to develop active lifestyles for improved health, but there is also an emphasis on gross and fine motor skills. Gross motor skills improve core strength, stability, coordination, and spatial awareness. Fine motor skills promote hand-eye coordination and will later help them with pencil control. Teachers may plan:

- Outdoor play
- Bikes/tricycles
- Obstacle courses
- Ball games
- Arts and crafts
- Sowing and threading
- Using small tools

Personal, social and emotional development

This area helps to shape their social world and ensure they are healthy and happy. Teachers create activities that enable children to feel safe. They work together on emotional regulation, a positive sense of self, and confidence in their abilities. Other skills include cooperation, making friends, and resolving conflicts. Children may:

- Make feelings jars
- Emotion sorting games
- Turn-taking games
- Drawing emotions
- All about me pictures and conversations
- Making good choices flashcards

Literacy

Literacy isn't just about a love for books and reading. It consists of language comprehension and word reading. Language comprehension starts from birth, as soon as parents begin talking to children and reading to them. Word reading begins later on as they start to pronounce words, decode printed words, and then with writing. Many literacy activities develop with communication and language activities. There might also be:

- Phonics learning
- High-frequency words flashcards
- CVC (consonant/vowel/consonant) words
- Literacy wall displays
- Initial sounds games

Mathematics

Bear in mind, they are only just coming out of their toddler stage, so they won't come home from preschool knowing their times' tables. They will work on numbers up to 10 and patterns found within numbers. At this age, it's more important to focus on a love for all things mathematical such as shapes, space, connections, spatial reasoning, and vocabulary related to maths. Activities can include:

- Find the missing numbers
- Do-to-dots
- Number hunts
- Counting and sorting
- Describing shapes
- Number playdough

Understanding the world

Children learn about places around the town, people we meet along with aspects of society, culture, the environment, and technology. Some preschools may organise school trips to support learning. Some preschools like to plan:

- Outdoor treasure hunts
- Gardening/planting seeds
- Role-play
- Celebrating cultural days
- Small world characters
- Recycling

Expressive arts and design

The opportunity to explore arts and design sparks creativity and imagination. It gives children even more chances to develop a wider range of vocabulary and learning concepts. Arts and design also help to reinforce learning about different cultures. The more materials children can access, the more opportunities for self-expression they have.

- Mixing colours and painting
- Designing hats or clothes
- Decorating Easter eggs
- Making snowflakes
- Seasonal activities (leaf painting)
- Making masks

Now, let's not get carried away here and please don't go to your preschool teacher and ask why they aren't doing all of these activities. These are just some of the things I have seen teachers prepare. In England, teachers have to make sure their planning covers all seven areas of learning but the actual activities they plan are not set out in the curriculum. This is great because they have the freedom to get creative and plan activities that are suitable for the class of children they have.

Rest assured, even though your little one will tell you they have done nothing, they will have had a day full of indoor and outdoor activities.

NAP TIME

For pre-preschool, there are often dedicated areas for little ones to sleep but from around 3 years old and preschool age, nap times tend to get fizzled out. If your child is only staying for one session, either in the morning or afternoon, there will obviously be no nap time.

For children who stay the whole day, they will have lunch at school and they are often encouraged to have quiet time after lunch. They might sit on mats or the carpet with a book and catch up on a little rest before the afternoon session starts.

INDOOR VS. OUTDOOR PLAY

In many preschools, activities are either child-initiated or adult-led. Adult led are those activities that are planned to ensure all the curriculum boxes are being ticked. These activities can be indoor, like cooking and experiments or outdoor activities such as treasure maps.

Child-initiated indoor play gives children the opportunity to choose what they want to play with, playing with small world toys, puzzles, role play, colouring or crafts, etc. Then, there is the final option of child-initiated outdoor play. The equipment will vary from preschool to preschool but common outdoor play activities include mini trampolines, climbing frames, slides, bikes and trikes, balls, and a sandpit, some may even have water activities.

Depending on the length of each session, it's nice to have a variety of indoor and outdoor activities, both adult-led and child-initiated.

SNACKS

The food children get will naturally depend on the hours that they are at preschool. Preschools can offer breakfast, a mid-morning snack, lunch, a mid-afternoon snack, and in some cases, dinner/tea. When it comes to the cost of these meals I can't quote a price. This is because the system of Universal Credit is a complex one, and it depends on individual circumstances. If you are in the UK, I strongly recommend looking into Universal Credit and what your child is entitled to and for other countries, find out from your local authorities.

Recently, I saw on social media how school meals vary from country to country, and it was quite interesting. Again, because of where I am based, I can give you examples of different food that is available to UK children with different menus each day.

- Breakfast: Various kinds of cereal with milk, fruit, crumpets, muffins, toasts, spreads, eggs, tomatoes, or mushrooms.
- Mid-morning snack: Fruit or vegetable slices, dips, breadsticks, rice cakes, or pitta bread.
- Lunch: A main meal with meat or fish and vegetables (vegetarian options) and a dairy or fruit-based dessert.

- Mid-afternoon snack: Fruit or vegetables, dips, oatcakes, plain popcorn, yoghurt, muffins, or cheese sticks.
- Dinner/Tea: Meat, fish, pasta, lentils, rice, fajitas, cous cous, soup with dairy or fruit-based dessert.

All meals come with water, and the snacks come with either water or milk. The reason why I have listed some of these ideas is so that you can start introducing different food types and this new routine as well.

Generally, there are two ways meals are served, and this will depend on the preschool. Some schools will have the more traditional approach, and all the children sit down and have their meals together. Others have what is known as rolling meals or snacks, and food is set out for children to take when they feel hungry. The happy medium is when various food is set out on the table, and the children can choose what they want to eat. As all options are healthy, parents are reassured that they are getting the right nutrients, and of course, children are more inclined to eat. This is particularly important for children who have difficulties with food, such as children with autism who have challenges eating certain foods. There will be more on this later.

MAKING FRIENDS

We have already seen how social and emotional development in early education is crucial regardless of where you are in the world. Teachers are well aware of the importance of your little one making friends.

According to research, friendships in the early years provide opportunities for children to practice social, cognitive, communicative, and emotional skills. These friendships help children feel secure and give them a sense of belonging, which reduces their stress. What's more, friendships help children adjust to different environments and improve their quality of life (Exchange Family Centre, 2019).

There are universal strategies that teachers use to foster friendship development in the classroom, starting with modelling friendship skills, giving compliments to children, celebrating important events, and showing concern when people are ill. Having a "classroom assistant" or helper of the day isn't because the teacher is lazy. It's because, in this moment, the helper interacts with all of the students, taking the register and handing out materials. Role-play, stories, and puppets are also techniques to teach the concept of friendship.

As part of the adult-led activities, teachers will include cooperative activities in pairs or small groups. Teachers are the most creative people and will often switch out traditional words of a song or rhyme and change it to a friendship activity, "If you're happy and you know it... dance with a friend!".

Sometimes, when it seems a child is finding it hard to make friends, they might set up a buddy system and pair this child with another child who has stronger friendship skills and similar interests. Again, there will be more on helping children make friends later on.

A TYPICAL DAY SOCIAL STORY AND COMIC STRIP

I have started my social story from when the child enters the class, but you can add previous steps if you feel it will help. It goes without saying that you can adapt the social story to a typical day that your little one will experience.

- Page 1: I will go into my classroom and take off my coat. I have my own peg to hang my coat on.
- Page 2: We will all sit in a circle. One of my friends will be the helper, or maybe it will be me.
- Page 3: We listen to a story. The teacher might ask some questions about the story.

- Page 4: After the story, the teacher will tell us that we can choose some toys to play with.
- Page 5: We have to tidy up the toys and put everything away.
- Page 6: We will wash our hands
- Page 7: The teacher will put some snacks on the table for us to eat.
- Page 8: When we finish our snack, we will be able to go outside to play.
- Page 9: First, we have to listen to the rules of the game.
- Page 10: Then we can play the game with our friends.
- Page: 11: There will be lots of things to do in the playground. We can play in the sand or ride a bike.
- Page 12: The teacher will tell us to line up, and we will go back to our classroom.
- Page 13: I will put my coat on and wait for Mum to collect me.

Even if children are only at preschool for 3 hours, that's a lot of potential conversations! I chose a comic strip conversation to help children learn how to share, take turns, and improve their friendship skills for this example.

Some children slide into this new routine with few issues. But considering how big a change it is for little people to wrap their minds around, it's perfectly normal for some children to need additional support. By preschool age, you may have seen some atypical signs with your child that are causing you concerns. You may have already seen your health visitor and are on your way to a diagnosis. In the following chapter, we will take a closer look at how learning delays and disorders can impact a child at this stage of their life and what support is available.

4

HELP AVAILABLE FOR CHILDREN WITH LEARNING DELAYS AND DISORDERS

If there is one thing all parents fall victim to and one point or another, it's comparing their child with others. This isn't because we think our children are better than others. For the most, we do this because of society's expectations and pressure. We do the same to ourselves, constantly looking at what others are achieving and wondering why we aren't living up to the same.

For the adult brain, this can be a good thing because it can motivate us to do more, aim for that career change or take that calculated risk. But when we look at our children and compare them to others, it can be unnecessary pressure on them and may have the opposite of the desired outcomes. As Albert Einstein said, "Everybody is a genius. But if you judge a fish by its ability to climb a tree, it will live its whole life believing it's stupid."

Every child is unique, special and has their own incredible skills and talents that are still, at this stage, at the earliest of development. Some children grow up in bilingual homes and start preschool, speaking two languages but are still wearing nappies and can't put their shoes on. Others can use a knife and fork to eat but can't tell you one colour from the next. And there are some children whose brains are wired in slightly different ways. This chapter is dedicated to those children who have or may have additional learning needs.

DELAYS AND DISORDERS THAT CAUSE CONCERN

As the focus of this book isn't to understand or diagnose, we will briefly look at the four areas where developmental delays and disorders occur. It's important to realise that in many cases, the cause of disorders and delays is unknown and rather than dwelling on this, early intervention is crucial. Personally, this is another good reason for children to go to preschool because professionals have more experience recognising symptoms.

This is particularly the case when it comes to cognitive delays. These delays can appear in children who have suffered from a brain injury, seizure disorders, or chromosomal disorders such as Down syndrome. But, there may also be cognitive delays that appear for no reason.

Motor delays can be either fine motor delays or gross motor delays. With fine motor delays, children may struggle to hold small objects because of the difficulties coordinating the muscles in their hands. When there are issues with large muscle coordination, children appear clumsy. Some motor delays come from genetic disorders like cerebral palsy and muscular dystrophy.

Social, emotional, and behavioural delays stem from differences in brain development and cause people to react differently to their environment. Children may struggle to read social cues, communicate, and cope with change. Situations can be so overwhelming that children appear to have a tantrum, but it's more like a meltdown. Examples of these neurobehavioural disorders are autism spectrum disorder (ASD) and attention deficit hyperactivity disorder (ADHD).

Speech delays can be expressive or receptive and will often appear together. Expressive delays are when children have problems expressing themselves. Their vocabulary may be limited for their age, and they struggle with complex sentences. For receptive delays, children can have problems understanding vocabulary and concepts. Speech delays can be caused by oral-motor problems (weak muscles in the mouth), brain damage, genetic syndromes, hearing loss, a lack of stimulation, or unknown causes.

Sometimes, there will be more than one delay or disorder. Or example, it is estimated that between 20 per cent and 60 per cent of children with ADHD have a specific learning disorder (Czamara et. al., 2013).

If you have any concerns, you should first speak to your doctor to begin the diagnosis process. This process may take a while, so you can also discuss your concerns with your child's new teacher.

EARLY INTERVENTION IS CRUCIAL

The sooner a delay or disorder is confirmed, the sooner the appropriate treatment or support can be provided. These delays and disorders won't disappear on their own. It is most likely that as the child grows up, their learning and behavioural differences will worsen. As they feel themselves falling further behind, they may become more frustrated, and their behaviour goes downhill.

In the first three years of a child's life, the neural connections in the brain are at their most adaptable.

When parents and professionals intervene in these years, it is easier to change these connections, which are the foundations for not only learning and behaviour but also health.

Different types of therapy are available, and a number of services can help children with their physical abilities, social skills, and ability to understand things. For those who aren't in school, your doctor or local authority will be able to offer more advice.

Within schools, there are dedicated educational professionals who work more closely with children who need additional support. In the UK, this person is the SENCO (special educational needs coordinator). It's a good idea to address any concerns you have with a preschool, even as early as your first visits. This intervention can have a huge impact on your little ones learning outcomes and, more importantly, their physical, emotional, and mental well-being.

WHAT ARE IEPS AND EHCPS

Individual Education Plans (IEPs) and Education, Health and Care Plans (EHCPs) are plans that document the additional needs a child has and what needs to be done for them to reach their full potential. The school's SENCO will help create these documents.

An IEP highlights a child's goals for the year and what support will be required to achieve them. Some common reasons for needing an IEP include physical disabilities, learning problems, speech, language, hearing, or vision problems, emotional disorders, developmental delays, and conditions like ADHD and ASD.

The first step begins with concerns from a parent, teacher, or doctor. Then, there is a team of people who will be involved in the diagnosis process. These people may include a psychologist, a physical therapist, a speech therapist, a special needs educator, or another type of specialist, depending on specific problems.

Next, the team, including the child's regular teacher and the parent or caregiver, will sit down and create the individual plan. In some cases, it might be that an extra teacher is in the classroom to support the child. In other cases, children will have classes in a special learning environment. Other elements of an IEP could be special equipment or modifications to standardised tests.

The main difference between an IEP and an EHCP is that with an IEP, the needs of the child can be met by the school. When these needs can't be met, an EHCP is created. An EHCP is a legal document that to put to the local council and highlights what support the authorities are obliged to put into place.

You don't need to have a diagnosis to create an IEP or an EHCP, but it's normal for the process to be underway. The special education need has to be identified, and typically, an EHCP is created once the needs in the IEP aren't being met.

It all sounds very overwhelming, and this is why parents work closely with the SENCO and the child's teacher when completing either plan. Don't feel like you have to navigate this on your own. Next, we will look at some of the additional support available to SEN children.

VISUAL SUPPORT

When words and communication are a massive issue for little people, visual aids can make so much difference. Once, I was working with a 4-year-old on the autism spectrum. He was vegetarian, and when hamburgers came up on the lunch menu, he would have a meltdown every time. The teacher explained the hamburger meltdown, and we started to look for what was triggering his upset. During circle time in the morning, the teacher would use visual aids to explain what was happening that day. The visual aid for lunch was always a hamburger. When the boy went for lunch on any other day when there wasn't a hamburger, he was fine. The day he saw a visual cue for a hamburger and a hamburger for lunch that he wasn't able to eat, he couldn't cope. By changing the visual aid for lunch to various food options, the boy's visual information was more accurate!

Visual supports provide children with another method of communication. These can be photos, signs, images, and even objects in the classroom that help children to understand different activities and the instructions that go with them. Having the day's plan as a visual aid on the classroom wall helps those children who struggle with change to transition from one activity to another.

Picture Exchange Communication System or PECS were originally created to help people with autism to communicate. It begins with an exchange of an image of something that a child wants. The child has a folder with a range of different images. If the child is thirsty, they learn to hand over the image of a drink instead of getting upset because an adult doesn't understand what they need.

This builds up to giving the child two images and asking them to choose which object they want. The next stage is to use the images in a basic sentence structure, "I want..." and the child adds the image. From here, children can learn other sentence structures like "I feel..." or "It is...".

Visual support will be something to discuss with the school's SENCO, but it is also a good idea to have the same visual supports at home for consistency.

AUDIO SUPPORT

Some hearing problems can be dealt with by a doctor, but it is also possible that your child will have to see an audiologist if hearing aids are required. Hearing aids work by increasing sound and making the sound clearer.

Before jumping into different hearing aids, there are some health conditions that cause loss of hearing; one of the most common is glue ear. Glue ear is when the middle ear fills up with fluid causing earache, ringing in the ear, or hearing loss. Sometimes, the glue ear will be monitored to see if it clears up by itself or with antibiotics. In other others, your GP might recommend grommets.

A grommet is a small tube that is inserted into the ear (a surgical process) that allows the fluid to drain. The tube falls out naturally within 6 to 12 months. Normally grommets or even temporary hearing aids are only used to treat glue ear when learning and development are affected.

There are three main parts to a hearing aid, a microphone, an amplifier, and a receiver. The microphone detects sound and converts the sound into electrical signals that are then amplified. The hearing aid converts the amplified energy signals back to sound, and the receiver sends the sound to the earpiece.

The most common type of hearing aid used by children is a behind-the-ear model. That doesn't mean to say that there aren't other types of hearing aids that could be more suitable for your little one. Here is a quick rundown of each in case you wanted to discuss alternatives with the audiologist.

Bone-conducting hearing aids

Instead of an electrical signal, BC hearing aids pick up sounds and transmit the vibrations through the bones of the skull and passed to the cochlea. Here, the vibrations are converted back to sound. It's a method that bypasses the outer and middle ear and therefore is used for children with conductive deafness (when sounds can't pass through the outer and middle ear).

Waterproof hearing aids

Most hearing aids have a water-resistant rating of IP57 or IP67, which means they can't actually be submerged in water. Hearing aids that can be worn in the bath and when swimming need a water-resistant rating of IP68.

Open-ear hearing aids

These are similar to behind-the-ear hearing aids. The main difference is that the receiver is at the end of a very fine tube which sits inside the ear. Having an open ear canal allows for a more natural sound. At the same time, this design means they aren't suitable for severe hearing loss.

In-the-ear hearing aid

This is one piece, small, with all of the components in one piece that fits inside the ear. It's convenient, but the child's ear canal has to be large enough for the hearing aid to stay in place. This is why it's not typically used for younger children.

CROS and BiCROS hearing aids

A CROS aid (contralateral routing of signal) is a device to help children who are deaf in just one ear. Rather than amplify the sound, it transfers sound from the deaf ear to the hearing ear so that children can still hear sounds from all directions. A BiCROS helps when the hearing ear has some level of deafness.

Vibrotactile aids

They can be worn by children with little to no hearing and helps give children a sense of loudness. A vibrotactile aid helps children to control their own voice by wearing a transducer against the skin (on the wrist or chest) to feel the vibrations of sound.

In some cases, hearing loss gets progressively worse, and hearing aids become less effective. Also, for children who are born deaf or become deaf before they learn to talk, an audiologist may recommend cochlear implants. The process requires surgery to implant a device in the inner ear that stimulates the hearing nerve.

There are some tips to help encourage your little one to wear their hearing devices. Hold them in your hands for a few minutes before you place them in their ear; it takes the chill off them. It's important to make sure wearing their hearing aid is part of a routine but it's best to start off with shorter times and build up on this. At first, you may need some distractions, at least when first putting them in.

Finally, get creative with your child's hearing devices. Get a bit of bejewelling going on and add some sparkle. I came across an awesome group called "Pimp my hearing aids/cochlear implants" for inspiration.

SIGN LANGUAGE VS MAKATON

There is a big difference between sign language and Makaton and their uses.

Sign language varies from region to region. Across the world, there are over 300 different sign languages. Even within one country, sign language can vary depending on grammar structure, accents and variations in language. Sign language is the language used by the deal community.

Makaton is signs that are used to support spoken language. It uses signs alongside speech to help children and even adults communicate. It's true that some signs are taken from sign language, but there are no variations for regions. So, sign language may vary across the UK, but Makaton doesn't. The other major difference is that as speech develops, the use of signs tends to fade out, but this isn't possible with sign language.

Because Makaton uses signs from the sign language of a particular country, it's important to find resources from your country. Even if you are from an English-speaking country, Makaton won't be the same.

Many schools include Makaton learning because it supports language learning for all children, not just those with delays and disorders, but it is not part of the EYFS curriculum. If you want to get started with Makaton in the UK, you can find Mr Tumble on CBeebies.

Or, you can join our Facebook community, Kids' Delayed Speech and Language Support Group and find Julie Pharo. She is our Makaton expert, both professionally and personally! If Julie can't find the answer, I know she is dedicated to finding someone who does.

Alternatively, contact me for information on my Toddler Chat course. Julie has contributed to the course, and there is a 30-minute video lesson that will get you started and much more!

A SOCIAL STORY AND COMIC STRIP FOR ADDITIONAL NEEDS

I felt that it was important here to have a social story that celebrates the differences within a classroom, whether that's cultural diversity or neurodiversity. Again, if you know anything about the children that will be attending class, you can include relatable examples.

- Page 1: Soon, I will be starting preschool
- Page 2: There will be lots of children in my class, and we will all be different.
- Page 3: We will have different coloured hair and eyes.
- Page 4: We will have different coloured skin.
- Page 5: Some children may speak a different language.
- Page 6: And some children may not speak at all.
- Page 7: Not all of the children will celebrate Christmas and Easter.
- Page: Some children celebrate Hanukkah or Eid al-Adha
- Page 7: Some children will need glasses to help them see.
- Page 8: Other children may need hearing aids to help them hear
- Page 9: Sometimes, children might get angry and upset.
- Page 10: And sometimes, there will be a special teacher to help children.
- Page 11: I will be a good friend and be kind to all the children in my class.

For my comic strip, I have chosen a conversation that introduces a child to the SENCO teacher.

Apart from introducing social stories, comic strip conversations, and visiting the preschool, there are still plenty of things that can help your little one make this big transition with as little disruption as possible. The following chapter is full of ideas that will help all children, not just those who have or may have a delay or disorder.

5

HOW TO PREPARE YOUR LITTLE ONE FOR PRESCHOOL

It's time to get more practical with our preparation. What we have looked at so far tends to focus on mental preparation for little ones. Now, we are going to look at changes that you can start making today that will introduce children to things they will face when they start preschool. Some things you may already be doing, and this is wonderful, others may need a little tweaking to get more benefits, and some might need a fresh start! There is time!

THE BEAUTY OF ROUTINE

Probably the most frequent piece of advice we are given (and give) as a new parent is the importance of routine. Rarely do we look at the reasons why both children and adults thrive on routine.

Routines help us to get on a schedule so that our body clocks fall into a natural rhythm, which helps with sleep, mealtimes and making sure we have the time to achieve all we need to. This is especially important for spending time together as a family and strengthening those bonds.

When a child is used to doing the same things at certain times of the day, expectations are established. You won't need to nag toddlers to pick up their toys when they know that is what needs to be done between play time and bath time, which creates a calmer home environment.

Finally, routines help us all to remember important things. For us, it could be paying the bills on certain days of the month. For little ones, routines help them to remember to wash their hands and clean their teeth.

It's more than likely that you have a routine established already. Now is a good time to start adjusting that routine slowly, so that your child knows what to expect when they start preschool. But slowly is the key, and this is why it's best to start earlier on.

As we have mentioned before, sleep is probably the first routine to change. At this point, you may feel they still need their afternoon nap, but you could start to shorten this time so that they are gradually going to bed earlier. Probably the hardest part is waking them up earlier, especially if this is a sacred time for you to get some other jobs done.

I remember with my daughter, trying to wake her up for preschool and never knowing which was better, leaving her to sleep as long as possible or getting her up so she had plenty of time to wake up slowly. It turned out that she wasn't ready for any type of breakfast for at least an hour after waking up. It's recommended that children at this age get between 10 and 13 hours of sleep, so you might need to work backwards to get the ideal bedtime.

After paying attention to her mood in the afternoons with 10, 11, 12, and 13 hours of sleep, I knew that 12 hours without a nap was our sweet spot. To get to preschool by 9, we had to leave the house at 8.40, so waking her up at 7 gave us plenty of time. We aimed to be in bed by 7. My other two children were completely different!

But this is the first place to start, trust me. Teaching independence and playtime are so much nicer when your little one isn't exhausted.

TEACHING INDEPENDENCE

This is such a funny one where parents can really have moments when they want to just pull their hair out, but it is an essential skill for preschool children. You are desperately trying to get out of the door on time, and your little one is taking 5 minutes to get their shoes on, only to have them on the wrong feet. If you do it, you can still make it on time; however, they will never learn. Then, when it comes to preschool and all the other children can put their shoes on, your child gets a knock to the confidence.

Linking this back into new routines, be sure to allow time for your children to be able to complete the tasks that they need to do. If, at this stage, it takes them 5 minutes to put their shoes on, give them the reminder at least 5 minutes before you need the shoes to be on! Every activity will take them longer than it does you, whether that's because they are mastering new skills or because they are easily distracted.

Despite their age, these little people are incredibly inquisitive and love exploring new things to do, and they also love finding ways to make their parents shine with pride. There are plenty of household chores that teach children how to work as part of a team and listen to instructions. Here are some age-appropriate household chores that preschool children can do:

- Put away their toys
- Put clothes in the laundry bin
- Water plants
- Feed pets
- Set the table
- Help put away the shopping
- Help with simple recipes
- Hang up their coat/ put shoes away
- Help sort the recycling
- Push the vacuum around

Bear in mind that these are all novel tasks for them, things that only "big" people get to do, so what are tiresome jobs that we have been doing for years are actually quite exciting for them.

When they succeed in their task, use lots of positive language. When they don't succeed at first, don't feel the need to rush in and take over. The goal isn't for the floor to be perfectly vacuumed; the goal is that they listen to the instructions, complete their task and feel confident. They don't need to be told they did it wrong. Positive language shouldn't be saved for the outcome, it should be used for the process. For example, "I love how you tried to put your coat on" or "I'm proud that you put all the knives and forks on the table" even if they aren't perfectly placed.

While teaching independence, think about the things they will need to do by themselves at school and focus on these tasks. Off the top of my head, the first will be pulling their trousers up and down so that they can go to the bathroom by themselves. This will be followed by feeling themselves, which will mean you need to accept some messy moments.

LEARNING HOW TO PLAY

There is nothing natural about our abilities to play. Little people have to learn the social rules around play time, sharing, turn-taking, respect and kindness. While these skills stay with us for life, the ability to just play is a tough one for adults. But if there are no other children for them to interact with, it's down to you to give your child the opportunities to learn how to play.

If you have read my other books, you may have learned how much of a fan I am of the cartoon Bluey. Bluey is an inspiration for children, but I think, more importantly, for parents because it reminds us of the need to play with our children and ideas to do so.

Play is how children learn to develop their motor skills, emotional skills, and cognitive skills. They also get to practice skills like enquiry, expression, experimentation, and teamwork. But this only happens when play is meaningful. The meaningful play has five factors:

- Children have a choice of what they want to do
- Play has to be fun
- It is more spontaneous rather than planned
- Play is led by what motivates the child
- There is a safe environment for children to experiment and try new ideas

There are some tips to make play more meaningful. It's important to start off by dedicating some time to play. This time has to be when you are not short of time or feeling pressured by responsibilities. It's crucial that there are no distractions like mobile phones or TVs.

Get down on the floor so that you are at their level. This will help to develop eye contact. At the same time, you want to make sure you are a few feet away from your little one. This space between you gives them the freedom to choose the toys they want.

Your role in the play is to engage but let them be the star of playtime. You can take the opportunity to reinforce vocabulary by saying what the child is doing, "Oh, you choose the blue brick" or "Your doll wants some juice". This is also the time to use positive language to encourage them.

The following games are some ideas that you can use if your child has a play date or things that you can do with your little one too. The most important thing is to work on sharing, teaching them how to take turns, and playing nicely. Signs of these skills should be positively reinforced.

- Sand: Sand sparks the beginnings of scientific learning. Poring and sifting show them how things work and improve muscles and coordination.
- Water: Water can be messy, making it a lot of fun. Similar to sand, it can teach basic science concepts and helps develop hand-eye coordination.
- Play dough: There are endless possibilities with play dough and creativity. It is also an activity that gets those tiny finger muscles working.
- Pasta threading: I like pasta threading for fine motor skills, but it's a great opportunity for turn-taking.
- Role play and dressing up: Children get to explore the adult world by dressing up as different characters and interacting socially. It gives them a chance to practice getting dressed.

- Character play: This can be with small world figures, superheroes, and dolls. These mini-figures help with social play and expressing emotions.
- Colouring and drawing- Children get to experiment with colours, improve pre-writing skills, and share colours with you or their friend.
- Blocks and jigsaws: These types of activities help with spatial thinking, logic, sorting, and organising.
- Outdoor play: It's a chance to burn energy, increase muscles, practice coordination, and improve confidence.
- Treasure/nature hunts: Children have to listen to instructions. They can also be given visual clues to support vocabulary, and with other children, they learn the importance of teamwork.

As you find the inner child in you, you will discover more ways to introduce play into everyday life. For example, counting how many times you can jump in a puddle or using the jungle gym at the park to create an adventure.

LEADING BY EXAMPLE WITH COMMUNICATION

There will be times when a child needs support from a qualified speech and language therapist. Until then, and even if you don't expect a speech and language delay or disorder, you can start using the Means, Reasons, and Opportunities model.

For children to communicate, they need a means. This can be through speech, but we have also seen that signs, symbols, facial expressions, and gestures are used as a means for children to communicate.

Next, they need an opportunity the communicate. Think of this as the when, where and with who. Opportunities include time and space, choices to make, and adults who are ready and willing to observe and respond.

Finally, they need a reason to communicate. Are they going to express their basic needs or feelings? Perhaps they want something or to tell or give you something.

Let's have a look at an example of how you can use means, reason, and opportunity to encourage communication.

Imagine you are in the kitchen, and you put milk on the table with them, but you have purposely not given them their cup. Your child has the means of communication by pointing to the milk or using some vocal means.

The reason for their communication is that they want to milk, but they need to communicate further with you in order to get the cup. Once your little one initiates the interaction, you can offer them a plate or a cup, giving them the opportunity to express what they need. Again, they may point, or they may use a word. Be sure to repeat the objects so they keep building up their vocabulary.

Because waiting times for a diagnosis and therapy are so long, I have created the Toddler Chat course with video lessons, weekly Q&A calls and free resources. Visit the http://kidssltessentials.com website for more information and to book a free 15-minute call with me so that we can work out how to get your little one on track. Join our Facebook group, Kids'Delayed Speech and Language Support Group, to contact me directly. You will also often find tons of information there and thousands of other parents that offer support.

DITCH THE DUMMY (PACIFIER)

If you haven't started to wean your little one off their pacifier by now, it really is time. Here are some motivating reasons why:

- Dummies can disrupt sleep, with children waking up just to find their comforter.
- Dummies can cause dental problems, especially when their baby teeth start to fall out.
- Dummies limit the opportunities a child has to speak after 12 months; the muscles in the mouth don't move as much as they should.
- Dummies have been associated with middle ear infections

Choose the right time to take away a dummy. It shouldn't be when they are sick or when there is a big event coming up. So again, start as soon as possible rather than just before preschool begins.

Start by trying to limit the amount of time the dummy is used during the day. Read stories about big children who don't need their dummies anymore. This is a nice way to prepare children for what is about to happen.

Some parents choose to use the Dummy Fairy. Together, you put the dummy under their pillow, and the next morning they discover a toy in place of the dummy. More often than not, it's a soft toy that becomes their new source of comfort.

GETTING EVERYONE INVOLVED

Realistically, independence, learning how to play and improving communication skills should all be weaved into the new routine. But it's not going to be effective if your child is only practising these new skills with you at home. They might not have the ability to transfer these skills when they meet their new teacher in a new environment.

Talk to other people in your little one's life. This could be the grandparents, aunts and uncles, and of course, any childminders you might be using. Let them know about the techniques you are using and why they are so important— more so if you are concerned about any atypical delays or disorders.

With consistency among all of the adults in their life and a routine that makes sense regardless of who they are with, there will be less risk of meltdowns and emotional turmoil.

USE A VISUAL CALENDAR

It might feel a little over the top, but considering the value of visual aids, having a preschool-sized calendar for the month enables children to see their routine on a larger scale. Include the days of the week so they have the opportunity to start recognising these words.

Quite often, preschools have a special activity for each day of the week. So you can link the day of the week with the planned preschool activity. It's important for children to be able to see that there is no school on Saturday and Sunday. It will also help to prepare children for when school holidays come up, and there will have to be a change in their routine.

TEACHING MANNERS WITH A SOCIAL STORY AND COMIC STRIP

I felt it was best here to deal with some difficult interactions a child may have when it comes to playtime and remind them how to play nicely. If we are being honest, even as adults, there are some things we hate to share, so it's understandable that children struggle.

- Page 1: At preschool, we will have time to play with any toy we want.
- Page 2: There will be puzzles, colours, dolls, books, puppets and lots more.
- Page 3: But the toys in the classroom are not mine. They will be for all the children.
- Page 4: Sometimes, I will want to play with the sand, and so will my friend.

- Page 5: My friend might be angry or sad because they want to play with all the sand.
- Page 6: This might make me sad and angry.
- Page 7: We have to remember that kind hands stay in our pockets, and it's not nice to hurt our friends.
- Page 8: If I feel angry, I will put my hands in my pockets.
- Page 9: I will use kind words and make sure we both have toys to play with.
- Page 10: If my friend doesn't like my idea, I won't get angry. I will tell my teacher.
- Page 11: The teacher will sometimes talk to the whole class and help us to learn how to be good friends.

Because this is such a challenging topic for them, my comic strip conversation will be on the same topic but will focus on what the two children say to each other during their time with a ball.

We have paid a lot of attention to helping children communicate but there is still one area of communication that should be touched on. You need to know how your little one is getting on in preschool and for this, there needs to be excellent communication between you and the school!

6

KEEPING UP THE COMMUNICATION

Communication is crucial on so many levels and not just for children. The communication that you have with both your child and the school is going to make or possibly break the progress made. It's true that, to an extent, this is going to apply more to atypical children, but that's not to say that all parents shouldn't be in regular contact with teachers.

Parent and teacher communication is vital to the success of all children. Teachers need parental input because it's the parents who know their children best. Communication provides opportunities for parents and teachers to bring up any concerns so that they can be addressed earlier. Above all, children are kept safe, and parents have more peace of mind. Parent-teacher communication is so important that Ofsted often requires evidence of a high level of communication throughout EYFS.

SUPER IMPORTANT COMMUNICATION

This really goes without saying, but when there is so much going on in your mind, it's easy to focus on all that has to be done, and the crucial bits get forgotten—trust me, I have been there!

First off, medication. If your child needs any medication, the school has to be informed. The school may need to see a prescription when necessary and educational providers may have to be trained in administering certain prescriptions. Prescribed and non-prescribed medication can only be given with a parent's written consent.

If your child has any allergies (and not just to food), you need to let the school know. This also applies to any special dietary needs or requirements.

THE USUAL LINES OF COMMUNICATION IN PRESCHOOL

Please bear in mind that this will vary from school to school, but there are some global communication methods that are common practice and not just in preschool. First off, the teacher will normally organise a meeting with all parents each term. This is a very general meeting where the teacher talks about what they will be doing during the term. This may include learning activities, school trips, and special occasions they plan to celebrate. Teachers will also try to schedule a one-on-one meeting with parents to talk about their child specifically.

Because there are so many working parents, it's not always easy to get to these meetings. It is worth seeing if another family member can go in your place or if another parent can "take notes". If you have a WhatsApp class group, somebody can share the information here. On some occasions, the teacher will send an email with a summary of what was said.

Speaking of emails, some teachers will use this as a form of sending general and individual information. They will also use this as a way for you to get in touch with them. Again, something important to remember is that during school hours, it's unlikely that they will have the time to check emails, and it's also not very fair to expect a response say, at 8 o´clock in the evening.

Because of the emphasis on parental participation in early years, you may have the opportunity to attend special events in school. If possible, take advantage of these moments because you can learn so much about how your little one is getting on by seeing them in their environment. School trips are so exciting for preschoolers, even if it is just a walk to the local park. Often, teachers may look for volunteers because the ratio of teachers to students will change. If it's a paid activity, you may have to contribute, but it is worth it.

Then there are the usual methods such as newsletters (digital and hard copies) and notice boards. Some teachers will have a daily notice board with a brief description of what the children did that day.

Of course, there is still the time you drop off and pick up your child, but it might be that there are 15 or more other parents all wanting to do the same. Teachers work to a pretty tight schedule and won't have the time to talk to each individual, but if you are really concerned, take this moment to ask for a meeting.

In the final year of EYFS, an Early Years Foundation Stage Profile (EYFSP) must be completed. This happens in the final term before they start the first year of school. The profile includes an overall picture of your child's knowledge, understanding, and abilities, as well as how ready they are for the next year. This profile can be used to talk about any concerns with the teacher and other teachers that are involved with their education.

MODERN WAYS TO COMMUNICATE WITH YOUR CHILD'S TEACHER

Since Covid, we have seen more and more technology in the classroom, which has been great for parent-teacher interactions. Some of these methods aren't exactly new, but they are definitely more popular now.

Most of us are huge fans of WhatsApp for its free ease of communication. Some schools will have a WhatsApp number where parents can send messages, and teachers may also share information about what the children have done. Because of privacy laws and data protection, care must always be taken. It's unlikely teachers will be able to share photos of group activities without prior permission.

Blogs and parent forums can offer a lot of information, and again, you will often find photos of children's work or the activities they have been doing. One of the most practical methods today is Tapestry. Tapestry is an online learning journal used throughout EYFS. It records a child's experiences, learning, and development with photos, videos, and diary entries uploaded by both educators and parents.

COMMUNICATION FOR THOSE WITH ADDITIONAL NEEDS

Your child doesn't need to have a delay or disorder to benefit from communication books. It might be that your little one is incredibly shy and has problems talking to their teacher, at least while they get to know the person. A communication book is a great way for parents to communicate with their children and the children to communicate with teachers and, of course, vice versa.

This book is a working process, so it might only start with a small selection of images, some photos of family members, typical daily activities, and frequently used objects. Choose a book or folder that is easy to pop in their bag or to carry but still large enough to have clear images.

Let's use some examples to see how a communication book can benefit everyone involved.

Typically, the teacher will start the day by asking everyone how they are. Someone who can't communicate or is very self-conscious can open their book and point to how they are feeling; the teacher can then respond with, "Oh, you are happy, that's great", or "You are tired, oh dear!". This way, the child can still participate in the class activity, and the teacher understands how they feel.

If a parent asks what their little one did that day and they don't have the vocal ability to let them know, it doesn't mean they don't want to communicate with you. By getting out their communication book, they can point to images of what they did that day and the snacks they ate. Much like the teacher, you would repeat the vocabulary that they point to.

If your child does have special needs teachers or additional support, it might be worth asking nicely if you can add photos of all the teachers they interact with. This way, you can find out more about what they did and the teacher they did it with.

As the child progresses with the communication book and you start to add more images, you can encourage them to start building longer sentences by pointing to different images, and you can use words like "after" and "then" to develop their language.

Try to provide as many opportunities as you can for your little one to use their communication book. This means it can be next to them during playtime or when you visit other people. The more comfortable they are using their book for basic communication, the easier it will be for them to develop their language and different communication functions, like responding to questions and commenting on things.

FINDING SUPPORT BY COMMUNICATING WITH OTHER PARENTS

It's a tough job being a parent, particularly at this stage of their lives. Despite millions of people being in the same boat, you may have moments when you feel completely alone, more so if you are a single parent or the parent who is responsible for getting your little one to preschool.

The other funny thing about parenting is that we never really like to let our guard down. We want to make it look as if everything is a breeze. If not, there is this cloud of failure hanging over us!

We tell ourselves that there is no competition with our little ones and that each individual child will learn and progress at their own pace. The same grace should be given to ourselves. We are all on different parenting paths, and these paths will have ups and downs at different times.

When you are going through a hard time, reach out to other parents because you will be surprised at how many will be feeling the same. There will always be that one who says life is dandy, but they might not be ready to let their guard down just yet. In all my ears in schools and as a speech and language therapist, I have never met a parent who can genuinely say they have everything under control and they have no concerns.

Parents who rely on each other and openly talk to each other have a massive advantage. Sharing stories means you end up sharing tips and tricks. Imagine, two mums are talking, one can't get their child to eat anything green, and the other can't get their child in the bath without more drama than Netflix. Mum number one says, "Have you tried getting a bag of bath salts? Don't know what it was with mine, but the idea of sprinkling some salts in the bath had them jumping in." Mum number two says, "Have you tried making pizza rainbows with them? Mine can't resist anything they have helped to cook themselves". All of a sudden, two mums go home to a much calmer evening!

Don't feel that you need to lean on parents in your child's class. This, too, has its advantages because you can share information about what is going on. However, there are numerous forums and groups that you can jump on to feel that you aren't alone.

HOW TO HELP LITTLE ONES COMMUNICATE WITH A SOCIAL STORY AND COMIC STRIP

It was hard to choose a particular area for communication, considering how vast the topic is. Nevertheless, I felt it was important for our social story to be about taking turns in a conversation and listening. A fast way for any parent to lose their patience is when little people interrupt…all the time!

- Page 1: At school, I will be able to talk to lots of friends and the teacher.
- Page 2: I can talk with my friends about what games we want to play.
- Page 3: It's important that we take turns talking.
- Page 4: My friend will finish their sentence.
- Page 5: Then it will be my turn to talk.
- Page 6: When my friend is talking, it is important for me to listen carefully to what they say.
- Page 7: I will try to understand if they are happy, sad, or angry.
- Page 8: It's important that I listen to the teacher too.
- Page 9: And take turns talking with the teacher.
- Page 10: Sometimes, the teacher will be talking to other people.

- Page 11: If I need to talk to the teacher, I will wait for my turn.
- Page 12: If it is important, I will raise my hand.
- Page 13: Or, I will put my hand on the teacher's hand so they know that I need them.
- Page 14: When we take turns talking, everybody is happier.

For me, the conversations these little people have are so important. The teacher won't always be there to play referee, so if we can start teaching them how to handle difficult situations the right way, there will be less risk of negative behaviour among the children. At the same time, we want to be able to discover as much as we can about our child's day without relying too heavily on the teacher. For this reason, our comic strip conversation is a fun "Yes/No" game to play with your little ones. If your child can't answer verbally, they can nod or shake their head or point to visual cues. Remember to paraphrase after.

Speaking of these negative behaviours, it is often mortifying to hear that your child has hit or kicked another child. Don't panic just yet. In the next chapter, we will take a brief look at these behaviours and how to eliminate them.

7

DEALING WITH UNPLEASANT BEHAVIOURAL ISSUES

Around this time, it's not unusual for children to act out in ways that you would never have expected. We know our little ones aren't perfect, but at the same time, getting called into the teacher's office because of behavioural issues could be enough to think you are raising a mini-psychopath but trust me, you aren't! These little people are dealing with new social and developmental problems, and they don't have the capacity to handle difficult situations in the right way.

You may even notice surprising outbursts at home. Some children pick up on habits other children have, the good and the bad. They might play a little rougher or have a new-found attitude. There might even be sudden refusals to eat food that typically had never been a problem.

In some situations, the behaviour will be related to emotional regulations, which is a subject that warrants its own chapter. Until then, let's take a look at some behavioural issues that may come up. Remember, it's not your fault and try really hard not to come down on them like a ton of bricks. This will require plenty of deep breaths and patience, but you know you can't fight fire with fire.

REFUSING TO TIDY

How many times a day do you have to retrieve things that have been thrown to every corner of the room and tidy up buckets of toys that were perfectly organised just 20 minutes ago. You wouldn't mind so much if there was some cooperation on their behalf. What's more frustrating is that one day they are more than happy to do it, but the next is just impossible.

Before the age of 3, children aren't capable of obeying, and if there have been moments when it seemed your little one paid attention to you, it might have been a coincidence that the outcome was what they also wanted. During these young years, they are obedient to their inner voice. The first stage of refusal, whether that's when tidying toys or any other regular habit they should be doing, is to do it together and model the behaviour you want to see.

The next stage you will see is that they start to obey more, but it's hard for them to do it all the time. This is where we introduce logical consequences. Punishments won't help because they aren't relevant to the behaviour you want to change. If they sit down in a time-out, how are they going to be motivated to tidy up?

A logical consequence is something that follows the sequence of their day. One of my daughters used to love cooking with me. Our routine was playtime and then preparing dinner. For us, the logical consequence of not tidying up was that she wouldn't be able to help me in the kitchen.

Really try to remember that they aren't being naughty or trying to wind you up, not even when they look at you with that defiant expression. It can take up to two years for their brains to fully develop the ability to follow your requests, so in that time, choose your battles wisely and avoid any power struggles.

THROWING THINGS

How is it that with no effort at all, your 3-year-old has the ability to throw a building block and of all the directions, it has to hit your head? Understand that throwing is a natural part of their development, but our job is to teach them what and when to throw.

Avoid saying things like "Don't throw that" as there is no guidance here. Instead, explain why they shouldn't throw that particular item. Is it because it could break and they wouldn't be able to play with it again, or could it break or manage something else, like knocking a picture off a wall or getting that little it too close to your computer? Also, explain how throwing things can hurt people and talk about the emotions that this may cause; somebody might feel sad or angry, even when it was an accident.

Provide opportunities for children to be able to throw things safely so they still have the opportunity to develop the necessary skills. This could be balls in the garden or foam aeroplanes; there are soft dartboard games that really can help improve their hand-eye coordination while burning off that excess energy. If there is no outdoor space, let your little one have a dedicated area in the home where they can use their "throwing toys". The safest place might be in their bedroom or just in the hallway.

TELLING LIES

Pre-schoolers might tell lies because they are exaggerating the truth or because they don't want to get in trouble. They may tell a lie to get something they want, and you might see this when one parent or caregiver says no, but the child tells the other that the answer was yes. They may also tell white lies so as not to hurt the feelings of someone.

For little people at this age, there is a fine line between fantasy and reality. They might lie because this line is blurred or to make their story more exciting. Avoid calling out these white lies or "tall tales" as they are part of their creativity.

At this early stage of their lives, the lies are normal and often relatively harmless, but it is a behaviour that you should aim to correct now before it develops into a bigger problem.

Don't call your child a liar. Child psychologist, Dr Carol Brady, says that the wound caused by labelling a child a liar can be bigger than the damage caused by the lie (Arky, 2022). Instead, find ways to talk about the truth in everyday conversations. This could be telling your child that the tree is blue and asking if that is a truth or a lie.

Take away opportunities where lies can be told. If someone has spilt a drink, you would normally ask if they had done it. For fear of getting into trouble, they would say it wasn't them. Instead, point out that there has been an accident and suggest you clean it up together. If they admit that it was them, use tons of positive language to show how proud you are that they admitted it. On a similar note, when you make mistakes, own up to them and speak the truth.

When children are more aware of the truth and a lie, and they know that there won't be negative repercussions, it's a good idea to give them opportunities to change their minds. If you have ever left a little one unattended in the bathroom, you may have walked in on one of those Andrex puppy moments with toilet role everywhere. If they tell you that they didn't do it, let them know that you are going to walk away and let them think about the truth, reminding them that an honest answer is more important than the behaviour.

If your child has ADHD or other impulsive tendencies, give them more time to think about their answer before you start to speak. These children may come up with an answer before processing the information, so your job is to help them slow down a little and process things before replying.

THE PRESCHOOL ATTITUDE

You may have thought that the attitude and back talk was only something parents have to deal with in teens, but I like to think the preschool attitude is Mother Nature's way of preparing us for the bigger attitude! Like with many behavioural challenges, when your little one comes back with things like "I told you" or "You do it", the first thing is to take a deep breath and stay calm.

This attitude is often a way of them testing the boundaries. If you have asked them to do something and they come back with a firm "No", they want to see how much they can get away with. Stay strong because if you give in, they will learn very quickly that your boundaries are flexible. Remind them of the tasks they are responsible for, repeat the instructions and stay with them until they have completed the task. If you pop off to check on something else, they are likely to get distracted.

Don't ignore the attitude! It's wise to let them know that their words and behaviour have consequences. Tell them that that is not a nice way to talk to people and ask them to try to repeat their sentence in a kinder way.

TEMPER TANTRUMS

Before digging into temper tantrums, remember there is a difference between a typical child throwing a tantrum and an atypical child having a meltdown (which we will discuss in the next chapter). A meltdown is when a child cannot cope with their surroundings either physically or emotionally.

A temper tantrum is when a child is tired, hungry, or not getting what they want, might be angry, want something, or feel that they aren't getting enough attention. Very often, at this age, they want to do something independently but can't, and this throws them into a rage.

It's easy at this moment to tell you to model behaviour and not throw tantrums yourself. In the heat of the moment, it's not always that simple. If you do have a moment when you haven't modelled the best behaviour, you can still model how to behave afterwards. Let your child see you taking steps to calm down and own up to your mistake. If you have raised your voice, apologise and explain why, clearly labelling your emotions without blaming others.

Again, I know it's hard, but try not to give in to the tantrum, even when you are in public. All eyes are on you, and you will feel judged, but how you respond to a tantrum goes back to your firm boundaries. The most typical example is in a supermarket when they want sweets, and you say no. Suddenly, there is screaming, legs and arms all over the place, may the odd insult from your little one about your parenting skills. If you give in on this occasion, they will do the same again next time.

Start by recognising their emotions, for example, "I can see that you are angry, but I need you to calm down if we are going to fix the problem together". If they calm down, reward them with lots of positive praise and let them know that when you finish what you are doing, they will be able to choose an activity or play with a special toy.

If they don't calm down, remove them from the situation. So if it's the supermarket, you would go back to the car until they calm down. It's frustrating, especially if you are on a tight schedule, but it's best to invest those extra few minutes now than repeat performances later. It is also essential that you go back and finish the task you were doing. If not, you are going to struggle to achieve any task with them, and that's impractical.

VIOLENCE OR AGGRESSION TOWARDS OTHERS

Let's get a few things straight here. If your child bites, hits, kicks, spits, or shows other signs of aggression, it does not mean you are a bad parent, and it does not mean they will grow up to be an aggressive person. The behaviour isn't always purposeful, either. It goes back to their developmental stages.

At around the age of 3, children have better motor control than they do language skills. When they get frustrated, they will use the "skills" they have to express their frustration. This isn't an excuse, and obviously, the behaviour has to be addressed, but from a parent's perspective, it's easier to keep your own calm when you appreciate that it might be the only way they know how to communicate at this point.

Whatever happens, don't retaliate with the same behaviour and spanking is widely considered ineffective and illegal in many countries. If you need to walk away for a minute, do so, but be sure to deal with the behaviour as soon as possible. In the moment of the behaviour, use short, simple phrases like "No biting" rather than a longer lecture where the message can be lost. Also, if you pay too much attention to the behaviour, you may end up reinforcing it.

Teach your child other non-verbal ways to express their frustration. Perhaps they can point to an image with PECS or in their communication book. You may also want to make a signal that you can use between you, even if it's something simple like a thumbs down.

Again, really focus on using positive language when your child starts to express their frustration in other ways, verbally or non-verbally. If you feel that there is no progress, it's worth reaching out to professionals (teachers or doctors) for additional help.

Before we look at our social story and comic strip, here is a short recap in the form of a checklist for behaviour we would like to eliminate.

- Don't push their limits when you know they are tired
- Be sure they aren't hungry or thirsty (take snacks out with you)
- Control your emotions- walk away if need be
- Always come back to address the issue
- Focus on finding a solution together instead of the behaviour
- Know your boundaries and stick to them
- Use logical consequences rather than unrelated punishments
- Talk about emotions and give them opportunities to express how they feel
- Know that this is not your fault and that this stage will pass
- Get help if you need it

REDUCING NEGATIVE BEHAVIOURS THROUGH SOCIAL STORIES AND COMIC STRIPS

Because aggression is a concern for many parents, the social story and comic strip conversation will give ideas on how to use these tools to help.

- Page 1: Hitting is when we use our hands to hurt someone.
- Page 2: Hitting is not OK
- Page 3: Sometimes in school, I will get angry with my friends.
- Page 4: But I can't hit them or hurt them in any other way.
- Page 5: My teacher has rules about hurting other children.
- Page 6: The rules make sure we are playing kindly and that we are happy.
- Page 7: If I get angry, I will put my hands in my pocket and walk away.
- Page 8: I will tell my teacher how I feel.
- Page 9: I will find an activity that helps me to calm down.
- Page 10: If someone hurts me, I might get angry.

- Page 11: It's OK to be angry, but it's not OK to hit or hurt them back.
- Page 12: If someone hurts me, I will walk away and tell my teacher.

For our comic strip conversation, we will take a look at a scenario at home where behaviour isn't as you had hoped.

Our final chapter is dedicated to helping our little people deal with these incredibly overwhelming feelings they are trying to work through. It's not just children with delays and disorders that need support in this area. It's important to remember that your child is an individual and understanding their unique triggers will help with emotional regulation.

8

DEALING WITH BIG EMOTIONS AND MELTDOWNS

Many of you would think that my passion is in speech and language therapy, and it truly is. But as you probably know, you need to keep developing your knowledge, whether that's for your career or other areas of life. If not, things start to become stale. I have dedicated my career to helping children communicate, but as you can imagine, one area that correlates with this on so many levels is emotional regulation.

It doesn't matter what I do as a professional or what you do as a parent; the most important thing we can do for children is to help them get good at recognising the huge range of emotions and how to control them. It's the foundation for social interactions and communication.

You know that when your emotions are in a mess, it makes it extremely hard to communicate, or at least communicate effectively. You might be angry, and things come out that you regret the minute you open your mouth or to the other extreme; you might be so happy and excited about something that you forget to read the temperature of the room, and your enthusiasm is totally inappropriate. Now, let's face it, we have all had a few more years to practice these skills than our children have had.

I have a couple of pointers that I think are really important before we get started, and I apologise to those who have read my other books where we have touched on these matters.

First of all, I think it's crucial that children are given the opportunity to express their feelings. Unfortunately, it won't always be at the most appropriate time for us. You can spend 30 minutes asking your child if they are okay and if they want to tell you something, but the minute you start that Zoom call with your coworkers, they tug on your arm, telling you that they are sad!

While there will be moments when you just can't drop everything, let them know that as soon as you finish what you are doing, you will be there for them—and keep that promise. There are two reasons for this. First, if you don't keep the promise, they simply aren't going to believe you the next time! Second, have you ever heard of the 'White Bear' problem?

For the rest of this section, I want you not to think of the white bear! We will come back to this!

The next pointer is that we, as adults, need to start getting better at teaching children that emotions are neither positive nor negative. They are just emotions, and they are all there for a reason. If someone feels ashamed or guilty, it's because they have done something wrong. If someone is scared, it's because they feel genuine fear, and if they are angry, it's because someone has wronged them.

There is nothing negative about these emotions, on the contrary, they can push us into taking action. We might need to apologise or talk about the wrongdoing to resolve an issue.

The reason these emotions are associated with negativity is that they can often cause negative behaviours. This is when we see our little ones acting out, as we spoke about before, and yes, the negative behaviour like hitting and biting. But for these little people to grow up with a healthy relationship with their emotions and the emotions of others, we can't afford to tell them that their emotions are "bad".

How did you get on with the white bear? Did the image keep popping up in your head? I hope my writing was so engaging that it didn't. But the white bear problem is a psychological process that happens when someone tries to deliberately not think about something, but the result is that they think about it more.

Adults get good at suppressing emotions, telling ourselves that we will deal with them "when we have time". Over time, we continue to push these emotions down until we pop! Children who feel that there are good and bad emotions are likely to suppress their feelings, and they will surface at some point. Not only that, but they start to ignore the important message that their feelings are trying to tell them.

GETTING GOOD AT EMOTIONAL AWARENESS AT HOME

Because emotional awareness has become such a hot topic for me, I made sure to include a whole lesson on it in my Toddler Chat course. This is one of the methods I teach parents in order to get better at promoting emotional awareness at home. It's a 6-step process that involves observing, watching, listening, interpreting, narrating, and goal achieving, or OWLING as I call it. I can't give away too much here, but you know how to reach me for more information on the course.

We have talked a lot about modelling behaviour, and of course, we can model emotional awareness, but only if, as adults, we can separate the emotion from the behaviour and accept that it's okay to experience a range of emotions.

Talking to a friend of mine, she had the most eye-opening experience when she learned how to stop raising her voice to her pre-schooler. She saw that it had absolutely no effect except to scare her little one, and this just started a chain of negative thoughts. Physically, her stress levels increased, her heart started pounding, and she couldn't focus on anything.

It felt like one of those "throw in the towel" moments, but the next time her child pushed her buttons, she just sat down and said, "I am sad, and I am angry". At this age, the first thing her little one said was, "Why?" and my friend was able to explain why. She gave herself an internal pat on the back for not losing her patience, but she didn't expect her little one to tidy her toys and come back and ask if she was happy now!

Sometimes we complicate parenthood to the extent that we tie ourselves up in knots, fearing that we are getting it all wrong. Sometimes, we just need to keep it simple!

Some of my favourite ways to help little people with recognising their emotions is through play. Naturally, puppets, toys, and role play provide opportunities to talk about different emotions and how characters might feel. You can also think outside the box.

There is a reason why the classic games stand the test of time. 'Simon Says' teaches listening skills, following directions, and if your directions are related to emotions, that's three skills with one stone, so to speak. Give instructions like "Simon says, pull a sad face" or "Simon says, pull a scared face".

Journaling has proven to be extremely beneficial for all ages, but of course, preschoolers aren't about to write about how they feel. What you can do is, on a piece of paper, draw seven boxes and write the days of the week in each box. Either with a pack of emoji stickers or your own pictures cut into smaller pieces, spend a couple of minutes each day finding the right emotion and stick it on the corresponding day. To extend the activity, you can have another box for you and explain why you feel the way you do.

Finally, you can make an adapted version of a flip book with emotions. Begin with a piece of paper and draw the outline of a face with hair, a neck, and ears. Take several pieces of paper and fold them in half, and pop a staple on either side to keep them in place. Now cut the folded paper to the size of your face on the A4 paper. Glue the outer pages onto the face. On the inner pages, draw different facial expressions to show emotions. You and your child will be able to flip through the faces, making up stories or talking about what might have happened for the character to react this way. You can also use it to encourage them to express how they feel.

WHAT CAUSES A MELTDOWN

We need to start with a little bit of science so we can understand the difference between a temper tantrum and a meltdown. In every situation we are in, the senses pick up immense amounts of information and feed the information to the brain. The brain then decides if the situation is safe or not.

If the brain perceives danger, the sympathetic nervous system kicks in. This is our fight, flight, or freeze mode. Heart rate increases, and breathing becomes faster to prepare the body to face the danger. On the other hand, if the senses tell the body that everything is okay, the parasympathetic nervous system remains in control. This is also known as rest and digest mode.

A meltdown is when the senses are bombarded to such an extent that the person can't cope. Things like bright lights, too much noise, strong smells, or even the touch of particular materials are enough to set off the parasympathetic nervous system. It's worth knowing that the parasympathetic and the sympathetic nervous systems are part of the autonomic nervous system, which means that it is completely automatic and not something we can control. This is crucial when understanding meltdowns because it's not bad behaviour; it can't be helped.

That's not to say we can't help the body return to the rest and digest mode. The tenth and longest of the cranial nerves is called the vagus nerve. Vagus means wandering in Latin, and this nerve does a fair bit of wandering in the body. It starts in the brain, passes the ear and the vocal cords, branches into many of our organs and then makes its way to the gut. This explains why we get butterflies in our stomachs or we feel sick when we are nervous.

Around 75 per cent of the nerve fibres in the parasympathetic system come from the vagus nerve. By stimulating the vagus nerve, we can help calm the body down. There is a very good reason why experts tell us to take a deep breath. Deep breathing stimulates the vagus nerve. So does splashing your face with cold water, so it's not just a fallacy. Because of the proximity to the vocal cords, things like singing and humming will also help to bring the body back to a calm state.

If your child is prone to meltdowns, it's a good idea to start by looking for the triggers and the early signs of a meltdown. This way, you can limit the amount of exposure to triggers they have. By spotting the early signs, you might be able to intervene. Because singing helps stimulate the vagus nerve, you and your child can have a favourite song to start singing.

If the singing doesn't help and a meltdown does happen, give them some space. If it's a sensory overload, the last thing they need is for you to push their senses further. As long as they as safe, give them space.

Of course, not all children will experience meltdowns but still suffer from stress and anxiety. Vagus nerve stimulation will still help with this but in the following section, we will look at some more ideas.

HOW TO HELP YOUR CHILD COPE WITH STRESS AND ANXIETY

Coping with stress and anxiety is similar to how we would handle other big emotions in the sense that we need to talk to children about it and not dismiss their feelings. It might seem that children don't have anything to stress about but in the case of starting preschool, there will be a lot of things that could be worrying them.

When you notice your little one showing signs of stress (crying, clinging, not being able to relax, etc.), notice and label the emotion without sounding like you are accusing them or putting them on the spot. Try phrases like "It seems you are upset about something" rather than "Why are you upset now?". Give them time to respond and actively listen to what they are telling you.

Validate their feelings, for example, "Yes, I can see why you are upset". Try to be specific about the emotions. If you can see they are frustrated, say frustrated instead of angry so they have the opportunity to learn more about their range of emotions.

As much as we want to solve their problems for them, try to come up with solutions to their stress and anxiety together. "How do you think we can solve the problem?". Naturally, you can give them ideas if they are struggling, just don't do all the work for them. Starting now will help them to grow up to be better problem solvers.

SEPARATION ANXIETY

Don't be surprised if you take your child to school the first day and everything is perfectly fine but on the second day they show signs of separation anxiety. On the second day they are more aware of the fact that you are leaving. Also, remember that separation anxiety often impacts parents more than it does children. When the teacher says that they were fine after 10 minutes, they aren't lying to you. However, the guilt and suffering you experience follow you throughout the whole day!

It's good to practice being apart before school starts, even if it's just 10 or 15 minutes at a time. This practice gives you the chance to create a goodbye ritual. Keep this ritual short and sweet. Dragging at a goodbye only makes it harder. During the goodbye, give them all of your attention and affection. Let them know that you will be back at a time they understand. Telling your little one you will be back at 3 o'clock isn't as clear for them as after lunch.

When it comes to the first few days of preschool, try to keep your morning routine as strict as possible. And, if you make a promise, like you will bring their favourite toy when you pick them up, be sure to take it!

Like so much at this age, separation anxiety is a phase and it will pass. Stick to your plan because you don't want separation anxiety to last longer than it has to.

MINDFULNESS AND MEDITATION FOR CHILDREN

Mindfulness can benefit children of all ages as well as adults. It's the practice of paying attention to the present moment and what you are feeling and what you notice around you. For children, mindfulness can increase focus, self-control, and compassion. They can do better in preschool, participating more and being able to resolve conflicts. It can also help reduce stress and improve behaviour. Mindfulness can be practised in a wide range of settings.

Meditation is a form of mindfulness. It allows people to become more self-aware by observing thoughts without judgement. Meditation can also reduce stress and increase focus but with other benefits like improved emotional regulation, empathy, and sleep.

Mindfulness for children is great because it doesn't require them to be still. There is a large emphasis on sensory exploration so if your child has any sensory issues, be aware of their triggers and choose alternatives.

Let's start with a mindful walk. Ask children to list as many things as they can see, hear, and smell. Find different things to touch and describe how they feel. You can add noise and movement matching to your walk too. Ask them to make a quiet noise as they walk slowly; the faster they start to move, the more noise they can make. While on your walk, collect some leaves and sticks to take home and paint.

Adding scents to everyday objects can increase a little one's curiosity and add a new dimension to playing. Add a couple of drops of essential oils to playdough or water to make a multi-sensory activity.

A mindful glitter jar is a lovely activity to teach children how to calm their thoughts. Fill a mason jar with water and add a couple of spoons of glitter. Screw the lid on tight and ask them to shake it. Leave the jar on a side for them to watch the glitter settle. Ask them to imagine that the glitter is their thoughts; at first, they are all busy and rushing around in their head. Slowly, the glitter and their thoughts start to settle.

You might think that preschool is too young for meditation, but it is definitely possible, especially as we aren't expecting long sessions. It's a good idea to try meditation after they have had some exercise or even just a little run-around. Ask them to sit in a comfortable position; you can get down to their level and do the same. The goal of your meditation session is just to spend a few minutes focusing on your breathing. There are some fun ways to teach breathing exercises instead of just counting breaths.

1. Imagine they are smelling flowers.
2. Sniff like a rabbit, three quick sniffs and exhale.
3. Pretend to blow out candles.
4. Pretend to blow bubbles slowly and gently.
5. Place their hand on their chest and the other on their stomach, ask them to take deep breaths and pay attention to their hands moving up and down.
6. Buzz like a bumblebee, inhale through the nose and, as they exhale, make a buzzing noise.
7. Snake breathing, similar to the bumblebee, but instead of buzzing, they hiss

To combine mindfulness with movement, kiddies yoga is awesome, and there are lots of free videos that you can do together. My personal favourites are from Cosmic Kids Yoga. The videos combine yoga with stories like The Hungry Caterpillar, and We're Going on A Bear Hunt. You can find them on Youtube!

ANGER MANAGEMENT THROUGH A SOCIAL STORY AND COMIC STRIP

There are so many books for children about emotional regulation, but I think social stories can be more beneficial if you are having a particular problem. Though our previous social story also dealt with anger, it was more about behaviour than managing anger. So we will look at this now.

- Page 1: Sometimes, things don't go the way I want.
- Page 2: This can make me angry.
- Page 3: When I am angry, I start to breathe quickly, and my heart starts to race.
- Page 4: I might feel like I want to shout or break something.
- Page 5: It's okay to be angry, but I have to control how I behave.
- Page 6: I will hold my hands.
- Page 7: I will take slow, deep breaths.
- Page 8: And I will count to 5
- Page 9: This will help me to calm down.
- Page 10: When I am calm, I will be able to think of a way to solve my problem.
- Page 11: If I can't think of a way to solve my problem, I can ask an adult for help.

For further help in dealing with angry pre-schoolers, the comic strip conversation is an example of how a parent might talk to their children when they are angry.

It takes ongoing practice for young children to recognize and manage their emotions, something that will probably continue for the whole of preschool. The good news is, now that you have mastered starting preschool, the same techniques can be used when your little one transitions to their first day of primary school!

CONCLUSION

Preschool is a wonderful opportunity for all children regardless of what has happened in the first few years of their lives. It gives them a chance to learn through playing and with access to tones of materials that they might not have access to at home. They can develop their creative and problem-solving skills, as well as fine and gross motor skills. They learn how to listen and follow directions, to share and take turns.

Above all, they get to interact with other children of the same age. This gives them the opportunities to develop their communication and social cues; two skill sets that are not only crucial for their academic years but for their entire future.

CONCLUSION

The transition can be a scary one, especially if a child has spent little time with other adults and children. But the benefits far outweigh the challenges that this change may bring about. But you have to get ahead of the process as soon as possible.

Don't feel that the only preschool is the one closest to you. It might be the case that this preschool ticks all of your boxes, but if it doesn't, look around. You need to be confident in your decision. If you aren't you run the risk of your little one picking up on your doubts. If you are concerned about any learning or behavioural delay or disorder, this is especially important. Even if you haven't got a diagnosis yet, the preschool you choose has to have the right facilities, staff, and knowledge to match the needs of your child. It might sound like you are asking too much, but you also need to have a good feeling about the school. If your child is going to be spending so much time there, you want to make sure it has that warm, caring atmosphere that encourages your child through the door.

As soon as you have picked the right preschool, it's time to start introducing your child to the idea that they will be starting school soon. Read stories or make your own and don't forget to start taking walks past the school at different times of the day so they can see what is happening.

Take the time leading up to preschool to work on the crucial skills that will help them at preschool and become more dependent. These skills include potty training, putting their shoes and coat on, feeding themselves, and tidying up. Arrange for some playdates if you can. Some of these play dates can be in your home so that you can watch how your child interacts with others and help them learn how to share and take turns. Other playdates could be at another parent's house so that you can start easing separation anxiety.

Any issues you pick up on during this time, you now have all the tools you need to make your own social stories and comic strip conversations. Of course, you can use mine but I really encourage you to personalize them as much as possible so that they are more relatable to your little one.

Although PECs and communication books have traditionally been used for children with autism, it doesn't mean that they aren't invaluable for any parent who wants to help their child with their communication skills. When a child can communicate even their basic needs by the time they meet their teacher, whether that's verbally or nonverbally, they won't feel so isolated in the classroom.

I have said this in every book so I can't break the tradition now. Play with your children, even if it is only 5 minutes a day. Switch off your phone and give them your undivided attention. Let them lead the play but be there for "vocal support" with phrases like "Wow, you are putting the blue block on top of the red block" so you are expanding their vocabulary. And have fun! It's healthy for adults to take these 5 minutes to get in touch with their inner child instead of being constantly stressed and worn out.

Apart from getting them prepared in terms of practical skills, it is equally important to start working on emotional regulation. You might be from the generation where we aren't good at talking about our feelings or that we are not supposed to display certain emotions like men aren't supposed to cry and women can't be assertive but in order to help our children, we need to break out of our emotional comfort zones.

All emotions are healthy and nobody regardless of age should be suppressing how they feel. Again, regardless of age, it's what we do with our emotions that become negative or positive. You can't expect little people to manage their anger if you aren't doing the same.

I know there is a lot of stress in your life and having a child of this age can throw you a few more obstacles, so I really encourage you to try mindfulness and meditation with your child but also, take an extra few minutes a day for your own practice. It really will lower your stress levels and help you cope with life in a more positive way.

On a similar note, reach out to others for support. No parent was born perfect and sometimes venting, and sharing your troubles and your successes is a great way to feel like you aren't alone and despite what you might think, you are actually doing a pretty fine job as a parent. Our Facebook Group, Kids' Delayed Speech and Language Support Group is waiting for you and you can find all the information you need about other books, my course, and to hear what other parents are going through.

To the faithful readers and the new, thank you so much for your support. It's with all my heart that I hope you have found the information here useful, practical, and straightforward. Starting preschool might be overwhelming but I promise it doesn't have to be. **I would be incredibly grateful if you could leave a short Amazon review**, firstly because I love hearing your opinions and secondly because your review can help other parents who are facing the same daunting experience.

Until next time, good luck with your little ones and keep playing!

Scan the QR code below for a quick review!

REFERENCES

Arky, B. (2022, April 14). *Why Kids Lie and What Parents Can Do About It*. Child Mind Institute. Retrieved from https://childmind.org/article/why-kids-lie/

Cadence Education. (2021, December 4). *Preschool Cost Breakdown: Average Tuition and Fees to Expect*. https://www.cadence-education.com/blog/parents-corner/how-much-does-preschool-cost/

Czamara, D., Tiler, C. M. T., & Kohlbock, G. (2013, May 27). *Children with ADHD Symptoms Have a Higher Risk for Reading, Spelling and Math Difficulties in the GINIplus and LISAplus Cohort Studies*. National Library of Medicine. https://www.ncbi.nlm.nih.gov/pmc/articles/PMC3664565/

Early childhood education and care initiatives. (n.d.). European Education Area. Retrieved October 17, 2022, from https://education.ec.europa.eu/education-levels/early-childhood-education-and-care/early-childhood-education-and-care-initiatives

Exchange Family Center. (2020, August 26). *The Benefits of Early Childhood Friendships and 3 Tips for Helping Your Child Establish Meaningful Friendships*. Retrieved from https://www.exchangefamilycenter.org/exchange-family-center-blog/2019/10/1/the-benefits-of-early-childhood-friendships-and-3-tips-for-helping-your-child-establish-meaningful-friendships

Free Early Childhood Education – Moving to New Zealand. (n.d.). Retrieved from https://www.enz.org/free-early-childhood-education.html

Hobbs, A., & Mutebi, N. (2021, April). *The Impact of Early Childhood Education and Care on Children's Outcomes, and the Sustainability of the Sector*. UK Parliament. https://post.parliament.uk/the-impact-of-early-childhood-education-and-care-on-childrens-outcomes/

List of International Preschool/Kindergarten in Asia. (n.d.). Education Destination Asia. Retrieved from https://educationdestinationasia.com/schools/preschool-kindergarten

www.ingramcontent.com/pod-product-compliance
Lightning Source LLC
Chambersburg PA
CBHW072058110526
44590CB00018B/3224